COUSIN VLADIMIR
&
SHOOTIN
THE CHA

David Mercer's new stage-play *Cousin Vladimir,* is scheduled for autumn 1978 production by the Royal Shakespeare Company at the Aldwych Theatre. Set in the Regent's Park home of Austin Proctor, a distinguished physicist and dipsomaniac, the play opens with the arrival from Moscow of Proctor, his new wife Katya and her cousin Vladimir. It emerges that the sole purpose of the marriage was to help Vladimir's defection from the Soviet Union, but, as he sobers up among his alcoholic cronies, Proctor begins to have second thoughts about his heroic self-sacrifice . . .

Also in the volume is *Shooting the Chandelier,* a BBC-TV Play of the Week with Denholm Elliott and Edward Fox. In Czechoslovakia in 1945 a Russian officer has to take over a country house, provoking a confrontation not only with the surviving inhabitants but also with a fellow soldier — in fact, his university professor. 'One of the most tightly constructed of Mercer's pieces' (*Sunday Times*), it is 'probably the best play for television that he has written' (*The Stage*).

The photograph on the front cover shows Denholm Elliott (left) as Simon Rusakov with Edward Fox as Colonel Nikolai Shchetkin in the BBC Television production of Shooting the Chandelier *and is reproduced by courtesy of the BBC. The photograph on the back cover is reproduced by courtesy of Irving Teitelbaum.*

David Mercer

COUSIN VLADIMIR
& SHOOTING THE CHANDELIER

EYRE METHUEN · LONDON

First published in 1978 by Eyre Methuen Ltd
11 New Fetter Lane, London EC4P 4EE
Copyright in both plays © 1978 by David Mercer
Set IBM Journal by 🅰 Tek-Art, Croydon, Surrey
Printed by Cox & Wyman Ltd, Fakenham, Norfolk

ISBN 0 413 39850 1 (Paperback)

COUSIN VLADIMIR

At the time of going to press, **Cousin Vladimir** was scheduled for first performance by the Royal Shakespeare Company at the Aldwych Theatre, London, in autumn 1978.

The characters are as follows:

AUSTIN PROCTOR, *a physicist,* 52

VLADIMIR KONSTANTIN RUSAKOV, *a physicist,* 64

KATYA PROCTOR (*née* RUSAKOV), *an English teacher, and Vladimir's cousin,* 36

HENRY CRAXTON, *an ex-army officer,* 58

GORDON, *an architect,* 55

SMIDGE, *his wife and office manager,* 49

GLENDA, *an actress,* 32

ANNIE, *a former cabaret singer,* 45

ALAN THORNTON, *a government scientist,* 68

PRINGLE, *a security officer,* 60

LEN, *a private detective,* 43

PART ONE

The walled garden of **AUSTIN PROCTOR**'s *house close to
Regent's Park, London. A hot summer's day. Time: the present.*

*It consists basically of a stretch of lawn which has been long
neglected, with trees, bushes, creepers etc., growing more or less
at random. On one side a small, green-painted garden shed. On
the other, a wooden gate in the wall.*

*There is cast-iron furniture — chairs and tables — once white,
now stained and showing signs of rust. There is also a wooden
table with a bench, on which stands an expensive tape-deck and
piles of cassettes. A small chess table with pieces. Rugs and large
cushions are strewn about.*

*At the back, wooden steps rise to a wooden platform and
glass doors which lead into the sitting-room of the house.*

Scene One

*We hear the heavy throbbing of a London taxi. It stops. The gate
swings open, and* PRINGLE *lumbers through carrying two large
suitcases. He is plumpish, spectacled, in a dark suit. He dumps
the cases on the grass and stands breathing heavily and looking
up at the house. He calls towards the gate:*

PRINGLE. Can you manage him, Mrs Proctor? I'm coming —

He goes out.

VLADIMIR KONSTANTIN RUSAKOV *comes through the
gate carrying a single suitcase and a briefcase. He is a thin,
gaunt man who looks older than his sixty-four years. His
stringy neck rises out of a yellow plaid scarf which is tucked
inside a long, black overcoat. He sits down in the nearest
chair.*

PRINGLE *and* KATYA *enter, supporting* AUSTIN
PROCTOR — *who is dead drunk in a glazed, aloof fashion.
He shakes them off and walks in an overcontrolled way to
sit at the wooden table. Closes his eyes.*

PRINGLE. Just a minute —

KATYA (*to* VALODYA *in Russian*). We must get him into the house.

VALODYA (*in Russian*). How?

PRINGLE *reappears with two more suitcases, letting the gate swing to behind him. He puts them down, to stand sweating and looking rather defeated.*

PRINGLE. I've asked the cab to wait. (*Pause.*) Till we get this sorted out.

KATYA. We don't wish to trouble you any further, Mr Pringle.

PRINGLE. It's no trouble. (*He goes to* AUSTIN.) It's his keys, isn't it? You've lost them, have you Proctor?

AUSTIN. Doors always open.

PRINGLE. Well how do you like that? And he brought us to the back. (*Looking at the steps.*) With all your luggage. (*Pause.*) God it's hot. We'll have to get you in. (*Pause.*) Wouldn't you be better without your overcoat, Mr Rusakov?

VALODYA. Thank you. I am cold.

PRINGLE *has found a handkerchief and is mopping himself. He takes in his surroundings.*

PRINGLE. Looks like quite a place. Quite a palazzo.

AUSTIN. Vodka!

PRINGLE. My God! After what he had on the plane!

KATYA. Please, Austin —

PRINGLE. Look. Shall we just get him inside? And then the bags. And —

AUSTIN (*without opening his eyes*). You see that garden shed —

PRINGLE. Yes —

AUSTIN. Well it isn't. It's a fridge.

KATYA. Please come into the house, Austin —

AUSTIN. It's a fridge. (*Pause.*) Full of booze. And glasses. And ice. (*Pause.*) And all that's nice.

PRINGLE *crosses to the shed and opens the door.*

PRINGLE. It is! (*Pause.*) Well I've never seen —

AUSTIN. So bring me a bloody vodka, will you?

Pause.

PRINGLE. Shall we all have a nice cooling drink? (*Pause.*) I
don't, myself. I wouldn't say no to a bitter lemon though.
(*At the shed.*) Remarkable —

KATYA. Please do what you wish, Mr Pringle. I am exhausted.
I go into the house if doors are open.

*She goes up the steps and tries the glass doors. They are open.
She goes in.* PRINGLE *disappears inside the shed and comes
out with a tray, vodka, bitter lemon, tonic water. He sets it
on the table and pours a vodka which* AUSTIN *takes, still
with his eyes closed.*

PRINGLE. What about you, Mr Rusakov?

VALODYA. Yes thank you. A vodka.

PRINGLE. Anything with?

VALODYA. No thank you.

PRINGLE *gives him a vodka and pours himself a bitter lemon.
He drinks it off and pours another. He begins to relax.*

PRINGLE. If I were Mrs Proctor I'd put him to bed when we get
him in. (*Pause.*) I should think you could all do with a bit of
rest. (*Looks at* AUSTIN.) Fancy bumping into Austin Proctor
in Vienna Airport of all places!

VALODYA. Mr Pringle —

PRINGLE. Yes?

VALODYA. You seem to have touch of fairy godmother with
those immigration men at airport —

PRINGLE. It must be thirty years. (*Pause.*) Well there's nothing
surprising about it. I do work at the Home Office, as I said.
And given the condition Proctor was in, it seemed only right
to lend a helping hand. (*Pause.*) Why do you ask? You were
all in order.

Pause.

VALODYA. No reason.

Pause.

PRINGLE. Well. I suppose we —

AUSTIN *bangs his glass down on the table.*

PRINGLE. Not another! I don't think you should, Proctor.

AUSTIN. Who the bloody hell are you, anyway? Damn well give me a drink —

PRINGLE half fills AUSTIN's empty glass. AUSTIN drinks it at once. He has not yet opened his eyes.

PRINGLE. No reason why he should remember me. It's a long time ago. (*Pours another bitter lemon.*) I hear about him from time to time. (*Pause.*) He's a bloody wreck, from drinking. I know that. (*Pause.*) Well it's none of my business, Rusakov. (*Grins suddenly.*) Shunted you in nice and quiet though, didn't we? (*Pause.*) I mean, I don't suppose you'd have been overjoyed if you'd had the press — and TV and all the rest of it. (*Pause.*) Not that they were there in the first place. (*Pause.*) A bit odd. They usually ferret things out. Still, it's lucky I was on hand. I'm a bit of an opera freak, you know. Been in Vienna for the opera. (*Pause.*) My wife hates it.

Pause.

VALODYA. Exactly what do you do at the Home Office, Mr Pringle?

PRINGLE. I'm a sort of clerk, Mr Rusakov. Just a poor down-trodden bleeding clerk. (*Looks at his watch.*) And it's after midday, and my wife'll have been expecting me in Ruislip an hour ago. Shall we get the bags in first and pour Proctor down the chimney after?

Pause.

VALODYA. Very well.

VALODYA takes his suitcase and briefcase, and goes up the steps. PRINGLE takes two of the suitcases and follows him. At the foot of the steps:

PRINGLE. I'll bet they're not having weather like this in Moscow —

VALODYA turns and looks down at him for a moment.

VALODYA. Leningrad.

PRINGLE (*nodding at* AUSTIN). Did you and your young cousin-did-you-say-she-was? Did you know what you were in for, with him? I was shocked when I saw him after all this time, I can tell you. He's paralytic with it!

Pause.

VALODYA. It has been good of you to help us, Mr Pringle.

KATYA has left one of the glass doors open, and he goes inside. PRINGLE heaves at the suitcases and puts a foot on the steps. He looks back at AUSTIN.

PRINGLE. That's most imaginative, that fridge, Proctor. Very imaginative indeed.

And he struggles up with the suitcases. As he goes into the house, AUSTIN opens his eyes and looks round. He picks up his glass and bangs it on the table.

AUSTIN. Vodka!

Fade out.

Scene Two

Fade in. *Mid-afternoon. The light in the garden is less glaring and more golden. We hear voices outside the gate. HENRY CRAXTON enters. Followed by: ANNIE, GORDON, SMIDGE, GLENDA and LEN.*

HENRY is a small, merry-looking chap with thinning white hair and a bald crown. He has a straggly, nicotine-stained moustache. GORDON, SMIDGE and LEN are dressed for the office: GLENDA in a shirt and jeans: ANNIE wears a lime-green summer dress with thin shoulder-straps — she is still thickly attractive, though bulging heavily in the dress and wearing precarious shoes. They are all more or less drunk, fresh from the pub, and already done in from the hundred-yard walk in the hot sun to the house. As they dispose themselves around the garden, HENRY goes to the garden shed and opens it with a flourish:

HENRY. Ladies and gentlemen, the bar is open.

He starts dispensing drinks from the shed, whilst ANNIE stands looking on provocatively. She launches into a few loud bars of a Piaf song, which are soon drowned by the noise of a passing jet. HENRY does not merely serve drinks, but bottles for those who want to go hard at it, a large bowl of ice, a tray with tonics, sodas, glasses.

ANNIE. Who says I can't sing?

GORDON (*pushing a drink at her*). Course you can Annie. Give us another.

ANNIE. I'd have been great, if I'd had a real chance. If I hadn't married that Danish ponce. (*Drinking.*) I sang all over Europe you know, with the band.

It is of course a routine. They have all heard each other's sorry fragments, complaints, private lives, a hundred times before. Being usually drunk it is doubtful however how much they remember — and each of them is dimly aware of this.

GORDON. Go on!

ANNIE. He screwed me up, all right. He did, Gordon.

GORDON. Get away!

ANNIE. Up yours.

SMIDGE (*vaguely*). When's Austin coming back, Henry?

HENRY. I've no idea.

SMIDGE. Well he's lucky to have you to take care of the place, that's all I can say. (*Drinking.*) Gordon and I've been burgled six times in two years.

GORDON. Smidge —

SMIDGE. Yes Gordon?

GORDON. Shut up.

SMIDGE. What did I say?

GORDON. Either shut up or get back to the office.

ANNIE. He wouldn't talk to me like that.

GORDON. You shut up as well.

ANNIE *puts her tongue out.* HENRY, *amiable and beaming, is looking round contentedly.* GLENDA *sits cross-legged beside* LEN, *who is stretched out flat, holding his glass on his chest.* GLENDA *laughs and raises her glass:*

GLENDA. Cheers —

SMIDGE. If I said something Gordon, I want to know. That's all.

GORDON. God she's awful. (*Pause.*) No. It's me. I'm drunk and *I'm* awful.

SMIDGE. Thank you.

GORDON (*bellowing*). Shut up!

HENRY. You can't beat a few in the garden after the pub, on a summer's day like this. (*Lifts his glass.*) We thank thee God for sending Austin, with booze and a garden for us all to get lost in.

SMIDGE (*to* GORDON). One of us ought to get back to the office. (*He quells her with a look, and she sips demurely.*) But it's such a lovely day. (*Dreamily.*) All those people out there in London working their fingers to the bone.

LEN. I'm supposed to be trailing some poor bugger's wife. (*Drinking.*) She gave me the slip this morning at Lords. What do you think about that? A faithless woman, at Lords. Does any of it make sense?

GORDON. Talking of infidelity. Who's having Annie this afternoon? (*Drinks.*) Our Henry?

HENRY. Oh now, wait a minute —

ANNIE. Piss off Gordon. Rotten sod.

LEN. God knows where she is now. I do know she hates cricket. (*Pause.*) Me first job in eight weeks!

GLENDA. I've only had one in five months. And that was a commercial.

GORDON (*singing at* GLENDA). Ring, telephone ring —

SMIDGE. I don't know how some people manage. When did you last have a job, Henry?

GORDON (*warningly*). Smidgey —

SMIDGE. Not that he needs one. What with Austin being so well off, and —

GORDON. I swear I'll do her in, one of these days.

SMIDGE. Well you've got a client coming in at five. (*To all and sundry.*) He doesn't care, you know.

GORDON *stumbles over to her and pours from his bottle into her glass until it spills over — and he still goes on pouring.*

GORDON. Now drink that, jelly-brain!

She meekly does so, and GORDON *crosses to* HENRY, *puts an arm round his shoulders.*

GORDON. Still no clue where old Austin's sloped off to?

HENRY. Foreign parts, I should think.

GORDON. Sexual parts, more likely.

SMIDGE. Call yourself an architect! He hasn't seen a drawing-board for years. (*Drinking.*) *He* can talk about sex. You ask Annie —

ANNIE. Now now Smidgey —

SMIDGE. Tartan underpants maketh not the man.

ANNIE. That's right darlin'. I bet he couldn't get it up if it was tied to a moon rocket.

GORDON. Ganging up, are we? We ladies?

HENRY. For God's sake don't let's all start quarrelling again. (*Pause.*) I wouldn't be surprised if that isn't why Austin took off for a bit. Us lot.

ANNIE. You treacherous little bugger!

GORDON. Who started inviting us here from the pub in the first place?

ANNIE. That's right it was bloody Austin, it was.

GORDON. I mean, there's plenty of places I can do my drinking you know Henry —

HENRY. I really didn't mean to imply —

ANNIE. He's a bit of a stuck-up bastard, anyway.

HENRY. Look, I honestly didn't mean —

GORDON (*stretching out*). Oh Christ, let's enjoy the sunshine.

HENRY *glumly moves round topping up people's drinks.*

HENRY. As a matter of fact we were thinking of trying to kick the booze, Austin and me.

ANNIE (*mimmicking*). Austin and me!

GORDON. Tell us another.

HENRY. Well. Cutting it down, you know.

GLENDA. Cutting it down to what? Mere cirrhosis level?

GORDON. I'll drink to that. (*Drinks.*)

LEN (*drinking*). Best of luck, then —

SMIDGE. Well we shouldn't encourage the poor man. (*Drinking.*)

Not if he and Austin have a little pact. A packsy-wacksy. (*Drinking.*) Ever so naughty.

They all guzzle reflectively at their drinks on this thought. ANNIE tries the Piaf again and is once more defeated by a jet. There are yawns and scratchings, vague peerings-about. ANNIE totters over to HENRY and touches his nose.

ANNIE. I bet Henry can't stop. Can-he wan-he? (*She sways, pushing her stomach out.*) I could just eat you up, Henry. I could straight. I love little bald fellers with pot bellies.

GLENDA. So Henry's a drunk. Austin's a drunk. We're all drunks. (*Drinking.*) Thank God we hardly ever remember what we've said, the day after.

GORDON. *I* am not a drunk, Glenda. (*Pause.*) I may be a *drinker*. That's another matter. But I have it well under control, thank you. Couldn't do business otherwise. (*Pause.*) I wish I could say the same for some of you —

Pause.

SMIDGE. When do we do business, Gordon?

GORDON. Shut up.

He turns to stalk away, and bumps into LEN — who is trying to get up. LEN falls flat on his body and stays that way. GORDON surveys the body.

GORDON. And what's more there's a bloke who can carry his too. (*Stirs LEN gently with his foot.*) The feller works damned hard and plays damned hard. (*Belches.*) When he's in work. (*Belches.*) We all do. (*Bends down to peer at LEN.*) Damn fine private detective, Len is. (*Pause.*) Look at him. He's worn out. (*Pause.*) Catch some of you tramping the streets on a hot day after some adulterous bitch with more cunt than brains! (*He turns away, suddenly indifferent, squinting into his glass.*) It's a miracle we keep Britain going at all.

SMIDGE. Your language, Gordon!

GORDON. But let's cheer up. The pound's steady, on and off. And so are the good old Brits if you ask me.

GLENDA. Even if both are a bit low.

GORDON stands over her to rebuke.

GORDON. And what the fuck do you know about economics? Or the British, for that matter? God damn it, you're not thirty yet are you? In my humble opinion, any person not old enough to remember the war can hardly be called British at all. (*Drinks.*) Especially a chit of an out-of-work actress, last seen grinning at some fool on the telly with a tonic water in his fist. (*Drinks.*) Let's face it, Glenda. If you're not up there with the stars by now, you're probably no bloody good and never will be.

GLENDA. Just concentrate on your own sense of failure, Gordon. I'm quite adjusted to mine.

GORDON. Failure? Me?

GORDON *rises and puts on a small performance, rather well.*

GLENDA. One of his more grandiose schemes in Spain during the sixties is still spoken of in awed tones. (GORDON *moves away with his back turned.*) Absolutely true. Hotels. A marina. Later known in the profession as the Costa del Ruin. (*Pause.*) And what about that block of holiday apartments in Portugal that fell down, sweeties? Actually fell down. On a lovely, bright blue, windless day. (*Pause.*) Haven't been back there since the Portuguese revolution, have you, Gordon? (*Drinks.*) It couldn't be shame. (*Drinks.*) Did you think they'd stuff a few red carnations up your arse, darling?

SMIDGE. He's nearly bankrupt, actually. (*Brightly.*) Doesn't let it get him down though, do you Gordon?

There is a silence. ANNIE *nervously starts humming.* LEN *crawls round filling glasses.* ANNIE's *voice tails away.* GORDON *comes towards* GLENDA *holding a bottle by the neck. He stands rigid.* GLENDA *suddenly proffers her glass. He bursts out laughing, and refills it.*

GLENDA. We're the hard core, girl, we are. That's what they call us in the pub. The Hard Core. Real drinkers. Professionals. (*Pause.*) Ten, fifteen years in the service, some of us. Eh, Henry? (*Looks up at the house.*) Well I mean, by comparison, Austin's only just joined. Eight months-? He's a novice. (*Turning away absently.*) Still, it's not the same here without him. Feels a bit like trespassing, you know.

SMIDGE. I really think Glenda ought to climb in the fridge and close the bleeding door.

She exits up the steps, with some difficulty, into the house.
GORDON *stands watching her. As she disappears:*

GORDON. Poor old Smidge. You wouldn't think it, she used to
be terrific in bed. Twenty years ago. (*Pause.*) Never been very
bright, of course. Didn't matter. Doesn't now. (*Pause.*) She's
so frightened of me walking out, she'll do anything. Any
bloody thing at all. Whip you. Be whipped. (*Drinks.*) Dunk it
in strawberry jam and lick it off for you —

HENRY. I say Gordon —

GORDON. What old son?

HENRY. That's going a bit far, you know.

GORDON. All those years in the army have addled your brain,
Henry. This is the Hard Core, boyo — not the pay corps. If
you can't take a bit of genial wife-bashing you shouldn't
have joined. (*He drains his glass and claps* HENRY *on the
shoulder.*) Ah well. Some might think you're a pouf, Henry.
But me — never.

HENRY *stares at him. There is one of the Hard Core's silences.*

HENRY. I thought one of you'd come out with that one, sooner
or later. (*Pause.*) But let me just point out. When I got thrown
out of my place dead broke, Austin was the only one of this
miserable bunch that did something practical. (*Pause.*) So he
took me in. So?

SMIDGE *is making her way down the steps carefully.*

SMIDGE. I've had a gorgeous wee-wee. (*Stops, listening.*) Listen
to the little pigeons. (*Coming to the bottom.*) I do think birds
are wonderful —

HENRY. I was literally on the street, Gordon.

SMIDGE. How on earth they manage to groom all those tiny
feathers —

GORDON. Calm down, little man. (*Placatingly.*) I didn't mean
anything. I'm a bit pissed, Henry, that's all.

SMIDGE *stands looking back at the house.*

SMIDGE. I don't know why he doesn't turn such a big house
into flats. Gordon's done some lovely conversions round here.
(*Starts looking for her glass.*) So convenient for the zoo —

GORDON. Why don't you bugger off round there? There'll be a

cage with your name on it.

But SMIDGE *is not listening. She has found her drink and is scrabbling at the lawn. She comes up with a daisy.*

SMIDGE. What a dear little flower!

She takes a glass from the table, pours some water in and puts the flower in the glass. She comes towards GORDON.

SMIDGE. Every petal a miracle of nature!

She holds it out to GORDON. *He takes the glass and throws it over his shoulder.* SMIDGE *bursts into tears.*

GORDON. Smidge lovey?

SMIDGE. What Gordon?

GORDON. Piss off and dig yourself another, will you?

SMIDGE *staggers away up the garden and goes to sit behind a tree.* LEN *has managed to get a cassette into the tape-deck. We hear softly, then a little louder: Marlene Dietrich singing 'Ich hab' noch einen Koffer in Berlin'. There is an air of nervous settling down, of collective self-aversion.*

GORDON. Berlin. (*Pause: then rousing himself, to* LEN.) Must we have that? Some of us are old enough to have fought the bloody Germans you know. (*Pause.*) Hey Len —

LEN. What?

GORDON. What do you think Glenda's like in bed?

GLENDA. You'll never find out.

GORDON. A fur-lined mousetrap, I should think. (*Pause: he clenches and unclenches his fist.*) An oyster with teeth? Grrrrrr —

SMIDGE *reappears from behind her tree, and totters towards the gate, sniffling at a handkerchief held to her nose.* GORDON *watches her departure approvingly.* ANNIE, LEN *and* GLENDA *are dozing off.* HENRY *is sulking over the chess pieces.*

GORDON. Client! You know what he wants, Henry? He wants a house on five floors converted into fifteen flatlets with a possible income of around four hundred a week. (*Pause.*) Henry? (*Pause.*) Still. One whiff of Smidge and he'll be too drunk to argue. (*Crosses to* HENRY, *filling his glass.*) Do you and Austin play chess then? (*Sits opposite* HENRY, *fingering a piece.*) Come off it, Henry. I know you went through a rotten patch. (*Pause.*) Not like him to just disappear though. Is it? (*Pause.*) Too pissed to move, usually.

Pause.

HENRY. He got a long telegram from somebody in Vienna. (*Pause.*) In German. It was in the hall one night when we got back from the pub. (*Pause.*) The next morning he'd gone. (*Pause.*) When I did his room there was an empty whisky bottle in his bed. I've never known him get quite that far before.

GORDON. When you come to think about it, we know bugger all about Austin. (*He grins, pretending to punch* HENRY's *nose.*) We don't speak German either, do we?

HENRY. Not a sausage. (*He grins weakly.*) Oh dear!

GORDON (*rising, staggering*). Well we know he's not short of brass. As they say up there in the dark Satanic mills. (*Pause.*) He once told me he used to be a physicist, before he came into the money. (*Checks his zip.*) We take *that* with a pinch of salt!

HENRY. He was, though.

GORDON. If I came into a fortune, I'd do some real work. (*Drinks.*) I wouldn't give it up. (*Staring at the trees.*) I'd try to *be* an architect. (*Hoots self-consciously at the thought.*) Look at that lot — (*Gestures at the others, dozing.*) The dead and the dying. What a contribution to the gross national product! Ah well. Pull yourself together, Gordon. Got to go and lick arseholes. (*He straightens his tie, brushes at his suit.*)

HENRY. I don't think Austin packed it in because he had a windfall —

GORDON. Henry.

HENRY. What?

GORDON. I genuinely don't give a fuck about Austin Proctor. He's a bloke I drink with. You are prattling, Henry. The Hard Core does have its rough and ready code, you know. (*Filling his glass.*) Did that sound convincing? That's my business manner.

Pause.

HENRY. He gets letters from Russia.

GORDON. Henry, old sport. I wouldn't care if he was the chairman of the Atomic Energy Authority and he'd defected to Moscow. What's needling you? You've got it cushy here, haven't you? Why rock the boat?

Pause.

HENRY. I think Austin's a very unhappy man.

GORDON. Now that *is* news for our merry little gang of teetotallers! Christ you're naive sometimes! D'you think we'd tolerate each other if we were *happy?* Be your age. There's a Hard Core in a lot of pubs. What unites the members? Drink. Strictly booze and nothing else. You're lucky. Austin can only be half way down — or you'd still be wandering the bloody streets. (*Going.*) Auf Wiedersehen, little man, and thank you for your owner's hospitality.

GORDON *drains his glass and weaves gently across the garden and out through the gate.* HENRY's *head sinks to his arm on the table, the chess pieces are brushed off. He looks down at the glass dangling in his left hand.* ANNIE *wakes up startled.*

ANNIE. I ought to go and get my kid out of school.

She crawls over the grass to fill her glass from the bottle beside HENRY's *chair.*

HENRY. Divorce him, Annie —

ANNIE. Can you see a court giving her in my charge?

HENRY. I've got to get out. I do live off Austin. It's a disgusting way to live, on somebody's generosity. I ought to pull myself together.

ANNIE. Pardon me, darlin', but there's still such a thing as work.

HENRY. After thirty-two years in the army and eight propping up the bar at the Fox? (*Pause.*) All they've got for me is clerical stuff. Forty quid a week if I'm lucky.

ANNIE. Oh? We've got our pride, 'ave we?

HENRY (*sitting up*). Not a shred.

ANNIE *hauls herself into the chair vacated by* GORDON.

ANNIE. Ought to get yourself a nice woman.

HENRY. All I want, Annie, is to chug through the remaining

years without too much bother. (*Pause.*) But what for,
I ask myself? (*Pause.*) Can you see Austin and me tottering
glass-in-hand into the sunset?

Pause.

ANNIE (*softly*). When did you last 'ave a bit, Henry?

Pause.

HENRY. Do I take you to mean — sex? (*He stands and bows to
her very unsteadily.*) Barrow-in-Furness. Nineteen sixty-four.

Rising, ANNIE *swaggers towards* HENRY *and stands with
her hands on her hips.*

ANNIE. What about it, huggy-tum?

HENRY. Oh, Annie!

ANNIE. I really fancy you, Henry. Straight.

Somewhat panic-stricken, HENRY *gazes up at the house. He
lifts his arms skywards, still clutching his glass.*

HENRY. How nice it would be to have a future. To know
where one was going to live and die. (*Pause.*) A nest. (*Drinks.*)
A cocoon. After life's great strategical disaster. (*Pause:
questioningly.*) A touch of security? Pull the pubic hair
over one's head and return to the waters? (*Pause.*) Ooooh,
Annie —

ANNIE. Race you into the house —

HENRY. I can't move —

ANNIE *swings him up into her arms as if he were a baby.*

ANNIE. Come on, den. Beddy-byes —

HENRY (*in mock alarm*). What's this?

ANNIE. Going to roll you into a little cigarette and smoke yer!

HENRY (*weakly*). Yippee —

ANNIE (*singing*). If I was the only girl in the world,
And you was the only boy — (*etc.*)

ANNIE *charges at the steps, and baulks at the last moment.
Still singing, she moves back and takes a second run. Her
momentum carries her up and through the doorway. There is
a last 'Yippee' from* HENRY *as we* **Fade out.**

Scene Three

Early evening. The few flowering bushes are luminous, the colours intense. The shadows under the trees are shot with beams of light as the angle of the sun changes. The afternoon's litter of bottles and glasses is everywhere. Only GLENDA *remains in the garden, still asleep in the fading light. She stirs. With a groan, she sits up running her hands through her hair. She finds a bottle and pours a whisky. The bottle rattles against the rim of the glass. She stands holding it in her trembling hands, then sips.*

VALODYA comes slowly down the steps, in a dark suit and black woollen shirt buttoned at the neck. He carries a stick and is self-absorbed. GLENDA *is in a shadow.* VALODYA *goes to the mess on the table and finds a vodka bottle and a clean glass. He pours one.* GLENDA *steps forward.*

GLENDA. Hello —

VALODYA. Good evening.

Pause.

GLENDA. And who might you be?

VALODYA (*smiling thinly*). Cousin Vladimir, so to say.

GLENDA. Whose cousin?

VALODYA. It is a little joke.

GLENDA. Whose joke?

Pause.

VALODYA. Forgive me. I am guest of Austin Proctor. Vladimir Konstantin Rusakov. (*Pause.*) Valodya —

GLENDA (*drinking*). Cheers Valodya. I'm Glenda Curtis. (*She gestures at the mess.*) Austin had quite a few guests this afternoon. (*She sits down, shaking.*) Excuse me. I'm in rather a bad way.

VALODYA. You are ill?

She holds up her glass. VALODYA *smiles.*

GLENDA. Have you and Austin just arrived?

VALODYA. Some hours ago from Vienna.

GLENDA. Christ! I'm surprised you didn't hear us. There was quite a gang. From the pub round the corner. (*She lifts her glass again.*) Drinking pals of Austin's.

VALODYA. We were very tired. And I think all soundly sleeping.

Pause.

GLENDA. All?

VALODYA. My young cousin Katya is with us.

GLENDA. You're Russian — (*Grinning.*) Are you a dissident?

VALODYA carefully hangs his stick on the back of a chair and sits down, after refilling his glass.

VALODYA. We shall clear decks, Miss Curtis. (*Drinks.*) I fall in love with you on sight. (*Drinks.*) In the thirties I was in my twenties. I saw what was going on in Soviet Union — I made my conclusions. (*Drinks.*) I decided human species psychologically unfit to perform as theory requires. (*Drinks.*) I imagine one who has kept his mouth shut ever since on this point can hardly attract your admiration.

Pause.

GLENDA. I thought Russians were supposed to drink their vodka straight off in one go —

VALODYA. Whatever this drink may be, it is as little vodka as I am Tolstoy.

GLENDA. Your English is marvellous —

VALODYA (*crossing to the table and pouring*). I worked beside an old Englishman for many years.

GLENDA. Where was that?

VALODYA: A place called Kolyma.

GLENDA. Never heard of it, I'm afraid.

Pause.

VALODYA (*gently*). Well so. You are Austin's friend too. And what do you do?

GLENDA. I'm a failed actress.

VALODYA. Failed so soon in life?

GLENDA. I'm a drunk. All his friends are drunks. (*Pause.*) Acquaintances, I should say. (*Drinks.*) I think I'd better get out of here —

She gets up, and half collapses towards the table. VALODYA is unexpectedly quick, and supports her. She pushes him off and sits again. Refills her glass.

GLENDA. Take no notice. I'm just unfit for human consumption.

VALODYA. Oh, could it not be worse?

GLENDA. That's a stupid thing to say.

VALODYA. Of course, you are right.

GLENDA. I suppose it's all so bloody rotten in Russia that we bloody Westerners had better not complain!

Pause.

VALODYA. You are ahead of me, Miss Curtis —

GLENDA. I'm sorry. I've been asleep. Passed out. (*Pause.*) And I get very — snappy. (*Pause.*) Until I've had a couple. (*Pause.*) And very frightened.

VALODYA. It is shakes.

GLENDA. Exactly.

She finishes her drink. Now VALODYA *refills her glass.* KATYA *comes out onto the wooden platform and calls out:*

KATYA. Valodya —

VALODYA (*in Russian*). Here —

She comes down into the garden.

VALODYA. I must present you. (*Pause.*) Katya, here is friend of Austin — Miss Glenda Curtis. (KATYA *shakes hands.*) My cousin Katya.

His glance has strayed to the glass doors, where AUSTIN *enters to make a very shaky descent down the steps. He is wearing the trousers from the suit we saw in Scene One, the same shirt, but no tie.*

GLENDA. Hi, Austin! Welcome back —

AUSTIN (*uncertainly*). Glenda —

He stands looking round at the mess in the garden. Glenda follows his gaze.

GLENDA. Just another workaday afternoon with the Hard Core —

He simply stares at her. She drinks nervously.

GLENDA. Had a nice trip? (*Wildly.*) All had a nice trip, have we?

KATYA *takes* AUSTIN's *arm and helps him to a chair.*

AUSTIN. Give me a drink, Glenda, will you? (*He looks from* VALODYA *to* KATYA.) They stare, you'll find out if you get to know them. They tend to bloody — stare.

GLENDA *reaches for a bottle, but* KATYA *beats her and gives* AUSTIN *a small whisky.*

GLENDA. He looks to me considerably worse than usual.

VALODYA. He just got married unexpectedly. And in Vienna too, which is by no means so romantic as it sounds.

GLENDA. Oh, bloody hell!

AUSTIN. That remains to be seen.

GLENDA (*to* KATYA). How brave of you to do it with Austin. Had you known him long?

Pause.

KATYA (*quietly*). It was an arrangement. A formality.

GLENDA. I didn't suppose it was passion. Not in his case.

AUSTIN. Women have always told me I'm another person when I'm drunk. Katya must've married the alter-Proctor. (*Drinks.*) If only I could keep track of him!

VALODYA. I will say, he drinks peacefully. All the way in plane from Vienna to your disgusting Heathrow.

AUSTIN (*filling his glass*). Watch out, Cousin Vladimir —

VALODYA. Maybe she should not have done it.

GLENDA. Shouldn't you?

VALODYA. It was for me. She is devoted to me.

GLENDA. Does she ever speak for herself?

KATYA *looks away, and sits with her hands folded in her lap.* AUSTIN *stares fixedly in front, constantly drinking.* VALODYA *goes to refill his glass, holding his stick sloped across one shoulder.*

VALODYA. I drink too. But not peacefully. (*Raising his glass.*) Like the very devil, as the great Wodehouse has it. (*Pokes* AUSTIN *gently in the stomach with his stick.*) But we Russians drink honestly. Everything above the board. Gross and foolish, but out in the open. (*Drinks.*) Austin, my dear

fellow. Speak to your friend Vladimir. To your Valodya.
(*Waves his hand before* AUSTIN's *eyes — no reaction.*) The
bloke is in shock, what? Far away. Doubtless in the land of
some inner torment. (*Beaming.*) As when in plane he refused
to go to lavatory. Said he was afraid of getting balls trapped
round axle while seated there.

*Chuckling, he sits by the chess table and begins to set up the
pieces.* GLENDA *crosses to* VALODYA *and stands looking
at him.*

GLENDA. I wouldn't marry anybody to increase your chances
of getting into this country. (*Looks from* KATYA *to*
AUSTIN *sourly.*) What've you got on the two of them?

VALODYA. Nothing.

GLENDA. Wasn't it rather a long shot?

Pause.

VALODYA. I am here.

GLENDA. I wouldn't have counted on your chances if you'd
been black.

VALODYA. I must admit, I have no heroic credentials.

GLENDA. Well well. Clever old Cousin Vladimir. (*To* KATYA.)
He said the 'cousin' bit's a joke.

KATYA. A kind of old family joke. (*Pause.*) Not very funny.

GLENDA (*looking at* VALODYA). I can see what you mean.

KATYA. It was a cruelty of my father's. (*She turns to blank*
AUSTIN *appealingly.*) I don't know what we are to do,
Austin. (*Pause.*) Austin —

VALODYA. Katya's father — my Cousin Alexei — decides when
we are still very young that Valodya is black sheep. (*Drinks.*)
Very stern moral chap, on surface. Could never see human
wood for Bolshevik trees. (*Pause.*) So he creates family legend.
Whenever there is trouble, it is *Cousin Vladimir's* fault.
I am kind of moral poltergeist. Something broken, lost,
stolen . . . some adultery or what have you . . . any kind of
monkey business in our district — why Valodya is at the
bottom of it. (*Drinks.*) Who else, among those pillars of
Soviet virtue? (*Drinks.*) And that is how little Katya and the
others were brought up to believe. Bloody strange, from my

point of view. But a sense of injustice is its own reward, don't
you think?

AUSTIN. Where's Henry?

GLENDA (*crossing to* AUSTIN). What *have* you been and gone
and done, old Austin?

AUSTIN. Get Henry. He'll sort it all out. (*Pause.*) I gave it up
you know.

GLENDA. What?

AUSTIN. Boozing.

GLENDA. You're on your way to being pissed out of your mind.

AUSTIN. That's one of the symptoms. (*Peering at* KATYA *and*
VALODYA.) How cosy to have one's family about one in a
time of crisis.

KATYA (*to* VALODYA). I think we must go on to Israel.

AUSTIN. Can you see him in Israel? (*Pause.*) I think his exit
visa must have been the fastest bit of bureaucratic juggling
in the history of the Soviet Union. You've got to hand it to
them. And I wouldn't be surprised if they've warned the
Israelis into the bargain. (*Drinks.*) He's the sort of person *any*
régime's glad to see the last of. If he were a Georgian or a
Tartar he'd have been shot.

GLENDA (*to* KATYA). I suppose you'll have had time to notice
he's an alcoholic?

AUSTIN. I am not an alcoholic. They can't give it up.

GLENDA (*crossing to* VALODYA). So what unlikely bond in
life have you two besides drinking?

VALODYA (*standing, posturing a little*). Austin and I once
belonged to that great company who, er — plumb? — yes
plumb the secrets of the atom. (*Drinks.*) Our respective social
systems being what they are, destiny took me to Siberia and
Austin to the consolation of the public house. (*Drinks.*)
Each must atone in his own fashion. (*Sits abruptly.*)

AUSTIN *claps.*

GLENDA (*to* KATYA). All I can say is, I hope you drink too!

KATYA. I prefer not.

GLENDA. It's tough shit all round, then. Isn't it?

She goes for another drink. AUSTIN *blearily spies a bedraggled and wild-looking* HENRY *coming down the steps into the garden.*

AUSTIN. *There's* Henry —

Ignoring them, HENRY *makes a ragged bee-line for the drinks in the 'fridge'.* AUSTIN *holds a finger to his lips.*

AUSTIN. Ssssssh —

They watch HENRY *pour a drink and down it. On the second one he begins to concede his surroundings.*

HENRY. Good God! It's himself! Am I glad to see you, Austin —

AUSTIN *heaves out of his chair and they fling their arms round each other.*

VALODYA. This dwarf is the incumbent lodger?

GLENDA. And what's our Henry been up to?

ANNIE *has followed* HENRY *out and is standing on the wooden platform looking down into the garden.*

ANNIE (*shouting*). I've been trying to make a man of 'im. But he couldn't find the way in if it was illuminated, could you, poor little sod? Well I'm off to the Fox. And if that's Austin I see down there you can come round an' bloody well buy me a drink. Bysie-bysie — (*Exits.*)

HENRY (*sitting shakily*). Oh friends, friends. (*Drinks.*) Gaw' — you won't believe it.

GLENDA. No?

HENRY. I woke up in bed with her, d'you see. (*Drinks.*) Awful. (*Drinks.*) What does she do, Austin? Grabs me by the John Thomas and starts singing. (*Drinks.*) Something from *La Traviata*, I think it was. (*Pause.*) Oh dear. Far from getting an erection, old boy — the frightened little thing sort of shied away. I do believe it actually retracted —

VALODYA. Is he a pederast?

HENRY. Have you ever been swung round a woman's head by the prick to an aria from *La Traviata*? (*To* AUSTIN.) Who is he, anyway?

VALODYA (*stands to bow ironically*). Vladimir Konstantin Rus —

HENRY. Oh yes? (*Turning to* AUSTIN.) Then she let off a

tremendous fart and went to sleep. (*Drinks.*) *I* can't find the way in? Ha!

VALODYA *crosses to the drinks. As he passes* HENRY:

VALODYA. When cat is away —

HENRY. Who is that feller?

GLENDA. Do let me introduce you to Austin's wife Katya, Henry. What would you say he is, Austin. Your non-paying guest? And that's Katya's Cousin Vladimir.

HENRY (*at* KATYA). His what?

AUSTIN (*putting an arm across* GLENDA's *shoulders*). My wife, Henry.

GLENDA. That's Katya over there, Austin darling —

AUSTIN (*transferring to* KATYA). My wife, you microscopic layabout. Got married in, er — where was it? Austria?

Moving, he intends to lean on the table but misses and sinks to the ground. HENRY *springs to help him up.*

HENRY (*dusting at* AUSTIN's *shirt*). Well you stupid bastard. Married. You'll never be able to kick the booze now. I don't believe it. Russians. It's a nightmare. (*Wagging a finger at* VALODYA.) Especially him.

VALODYA. I can see in one respect Britain very like Soviet Union —

HENRY. Impossible —

VALODYA. Everybody drunk.

HENRY *is chewing his ragged little moustache and trying to reassemble his wits.*

HENRY. I wouldn't say that — Rookarseoff is it?

VALODYA. Fortunately is big house. Plenty of room for all.

HENRY *is alerted by this, and slowly walks round* VALODYA *inspecting him. Then with a glance from* KATYA *to* AUSTIN:

HENRY. You would damn well go off abroad on your own, wouldn't you?

AUSTIN. I hardly remember a thing.

There is an uneasy silence. KATYA *is distressed and fighting down panic.*

KATYA. You should eat something, Austin. I will go and see what there is.

Slowly, she turns and goes towards the steps. All except AUSTIN *watch her go into the house.*

AUSTIN. Henry and I don't eat.

GLENDA. Well *I* feel shitty. If nobody else does.

AUSTIN. Speaking for myself. (*Pause.*) Nothing can ruffle my huge sense of inadequacy.

Pause.

VALODYA. Would you be kind to her, Austin?

AUSTIN *stares at him a moment, then goes into the house staggering a little — and keeping his glass.* HENRY *reaches for* VALODYA's *glass.*

HENRY. Vodka, was it?

VALODYA. Approximately.

HENRY *goes to the garden shed 'fridge' and brings out a bottle of whisky and one of vodka. He refills* GLENDA's *glass, then* VALODYA's — *gesturing at the shed.*

HENRY. How about that — eh?

VALODYA. Stalin would have been fascinated.

HENRY. Let me just try to put you in the picture.

VALODYA. Are you in it?

HENRY. Well I've been living here for some time, you know.

GLENDA. That's to say he and Austin sleep here when they're not in the pub.

HENRY. And Glenda had her aspirations, too.

VALODYA. How did you know my name is Rusakov, Henry?

Pause.

HENRY. Did I?

VALODYA. You made play on words with it. (*Pause.*) Rookarseoff?

Pause.

HENRY. You introduced yourself —

VALODYA. Almost.

HENRY. Spare us the paranoia. This isn't Russia, you know.

Pause.

VALODYA. In Soviet Union, what we all fear — very often happens.

HENRY. D'you think we don't know what's going on over there?

VALODYA. I am sure you do.

HENRY. I had my bellyfull in Korea.

GLENDA. Would you be here now if it weren't for the stink kicked up in the West about repression? Come on!

VALODYA. I told you I —

GLENDA. But you see Henry, Cousin Vladimir *isn't* a dissident. He told me. (*Pause.*) I wonder what he is?

HENRY (*drinking, he throws an accusatory arm*). Confess!

VALODYA. Why are you so hostile, Miss Curtis?

GLENDA. Well it would have been quite interesting. To meet a man with some guts for a change. (*Drinks.*) Pity. (*Drinks.*) I thought I hadn't seen your name in the papers.

Pause.

VALODYA. I am one Russian who is a little tired of the outcry in the West. (*Goes to refill his glass.*) Do not misunderstand me. (*Drinks.*) I think there are many brave men and women in my country who are grateful. (*Drinks.*) It has surely reduced the sufferings of a few. It has secured the release of some. Our authorities are indeed sensitive to it. (*Drinks.*) All this is true. But —

GLENDA. But speaking personally, you'd lived with your mouth shut and it didn't help you?

Pause.

VALODYA. I sometimes think this loud moral crusade . . . is also welcome diversion from your terrible apathy towards your own predicament. Your own society.

HENRY *is quite drunk by now, and gestures vaguely at the mess left behind by the Hard Core, at the house, at the trees.*

HENRY. Oh I say! I wouldn't like you to get the mistaken

impression that this is England! (*Drinks.*) Our sordid little corner —

VALODYA. You are patriot, Henry? (*Drinks.*) How charming.

GLENDA (*turning away*). He's disgusting.

HENRY. I think he probably is.

VALODYA. Excuse me. I understand your position.

HENRY (*drinking*). Shrewd feller!

VALODYA. I am looking for comfortable niche myself, this twenty years.

HENRY. You bastard!

VALODYA (*sighing*). Is time to settle down. (*Pause.*) Damned informers and busybodies like ants, in Soviet Union. Fifty roubles here, hundred roubles there. In England I understand you have taxes. In Russia, businessman faces pure naked avarice, Henry. So depressing.

Pause.

HENRY. Business?

VALODYA (*vaguely*). In a small way. (*Pause.*) But Henry, please believe it. Austin has said this is your home.

GLENDA. I thought you said you were a scientist.

VALODYA. A long time ago. Before labour camp.

HENRY (*highly impressed*). You were in the Gulag?

VALODYA. Please remove idiotic look of respect from your face, Henry. (*Pause.*) Is not some kind of ideological oscar.

HENRY. We've all read our Solzhenitsyn, you know.

VALODYA. Ah well. You must forgive me for being merely Rusakov. (*Drinks.*) Do try —

GLENDA. Can you?

VALODYA (*stands and bows*). Blasphemous to utter the names Rusakov and Solzhenitsyn in same breath. (*Sitting.*) It does not matter if he writes like a monkey who has read *War and Peace*. In moral universe he is a great man. (*Drinks.*) What a pity Russians have to suffer, before West discovers it has no monopoly of truth and dignity. (*Drinks.*) In my youth in the thirties, the silence from this part of the world was deafening.

(*Drinks.*) Could it be the children of the fellow-travellers are now ashamed of their fathers?

HENRY. 's all a bit beyond me, old man. (*Drinks.*) Just thank your lucky stars you're in England. I don't care what they say. We may be down at heel, (*Drinks.*) but you're still better off here than just about anywhere else in the world. (*Reflecting.*) Licensing hours a touch on the vindictive side —

GLENDA. I do believe Austin keeps him here as some kind of pet!

HENRY. Tha's right. Funny hopeless Henry. (*Lurching for the bottle.*) One thing I do know. I've had *La Traviata*. (*Pouring.*) For ever!

GLENDA. So why are you running if it's not political?

HENRY. Course it's political!

VALODYA. He is right. I loathe Soviet system and I wish to be out. (*Drinks.*) I am heretic. (*Drinks.*) I suffer from conviction that what our Marxists call 'bourgeois freedom' — is also freedom!

HENRY (*glumly*). I've never felt so damned bloody free in all my life as I have lately. (*Drinks.*) Haven't the faintest idea what to do with myself. (*He rounds on* VALODYA *fiercely.*) Did you push that young woman into marrying Austin?

Pause.

VALODYA. A very long time ago Austin was in Leningrad with a British scientific delegation. Someone brought us together because he wanted to meet me. (*Pause.*) He had read a paper of mine in his own field. (*Pause.*) He admired it and did not understand then why I was ostracised. (*Pause.*) In those days we found a great respect for each other. (*Drinks.*) Neither of us drank much, at this time —

HENRY. Pen-pals! It's you he's been writing to —

VALODYA. Letters of whisky and tears. Life ruined. Wishes to commit suicide. Has not the courage. Guilt. Rage. Impotent screams of self-pity. (*Drinks.*) I smile to myself at this preposterous Englishman. He has two hundred thousand quids, has he not. ((*Pause.*) (*Drinks.*) No broken marriage. No tragic affair, or whatever. No social disgrace. Envied in his scientific work. Heads for Nobel Prize. (*Drinks.*) How I envied this via Dolorosa!

HENRY. Oh, come now —

VALODYA. Money and agony not mutually exclusive? Quite so, Henry. Austin's tone menopausal, I thought. But we have been colleagues, friends a little. Is normal for neurotics to unburden their suffering to Cousin Vladimir. Extraordinary. If I am drowning, some fool would pull me out to tell me his life story.

HENRY. Austin a neurotic? Seems a perfectly ordinary sort of drunk to me.

VALODYA. It is no doubt Russian weakness to regard as aberration in others what they wish to ignore in themselves. Our psychiatrists brilliant in this way. Some chatterbox dreams of God, freedom — you don't say, Comrade! Well well well. Looks to me like you need an injection. What's that? Is people following you and insulting you? My dear fellow, it doesn't happen under socialism. Grigori, pass me the strait-jacket —

GLENDA. So what's a few pissy letters, for God's sake?

VALODYA. If Austin Soviet citizen, he could be in trouble. According to some of our top men, Miss Curtis — there is astonishing mental phenomenon called 'creeping schizophrenia'. Some people get funny ideas, look around, start thinking. Open their mouths. And bim-bam, the inside of their heads is in trouble. (*Drinks.*) Creeping schizophrenia. (*Drinks.*) It means you are so damn crazy you don't even know it.

VALODYA *refills his glass and walks about the garden. He touches one flower, sniffs another, picks another and puts it in his lapel.*

VALODYA. I am in England — in London! (*Drinks.*) Such a beautiful house. Such a garden. (*He breathes deeply and looks up at the house.*) So many rooms! Bathrooms, bedrooms. Bidets for passing ladies. (*He approaches* GLENDA *and stands looking at her.*) In Vienna, Katya and I quarrelled. (*Pause.*) I get drunk. I send telegram to Austin. (*Drinks.*) Who am I to see disaster rising out of farce? (*Drinks.*) Katya is in a kind of shock from coming out. (*Drinks.*) After all, her father — my stupid Cousin Alexei — is in K.G.B. (*Drinks.*) None of it makes sense —

GLENDA. You're damn right it doesn't! Your fantasy life's worse than Austin's.

VALODYA. Oh, Alexei is not really a bad fellow. Just a born lackey. (*Drinks.*) Not all our secret policemen are thugs or careerists. A proportion is genuinely dumb.

GLENDA. I know what it is. He's a dissident inside his head. (*Pause.*) That's just how my grandfather lived with his communism. He was all for revolution, so long as it happened extremely far away and involved only foreigners. (*Drinks.*) The old hypocrite kept it up right until the invasion of Czechoslovakia. Then he announced that maybe social democracy is the last bulwark of individual freedom — and promptly died to underline his grief.

VALODYA. Ah, Glenda. I must call you Glenda as I have fallen in love. I am sucker for bitchy women. (*Drinks.*) We were visited by hundreds of Glenda-grandfathers. They came. They saw. They were conquered. (*Drinks.*) You are right. They were ecstatic about social system they would not tolerate for one day at home. (*Drinks.*) The Cousin Vladimirs of this world stood by with frozen smiles, and incredulity in their hearts. Children, we thought. (*Drinks.*) They had rational justification for all our sufferings. Our 'objective conditions' required stern measures. (*Drinks.*) Oh my God, what a stream of political imbeciles wined and dined their way through Soviet Russia! (*Drinks.*) Children! Babies! (*Drinks.*) How hungry they were to believe. (*Pause.*) It is sad. (*Drinks.*) How they needed this hope of the Bolshevik Revolution! (*Pause.*) I do understand it.

Pause.

GLENDA. What you mean is: the Cousin Vladimirs had one priority. To save their own necks. (*Drinks.*) And now a rat like you scuttles out, leaving better men and women to go to prison and into the mental hospitals for you. (*Drinks.*) If Austin weren't smashed rotten from morning till night he'd have told you to go to hell. (*Shouting.*) I'm telling you to go to hell! (*As she makes for the gate.*) I feel degraded being near you — (*Exits.*)

Pause.

VALODYA (*looking at his glass*). This vodka is truly dog's piss.

HENRY. She shouldn't have gone for you like that. (*Pause.*) She's got some pretty stark problems of her own.

VALODYA. She is in love with Austin?

HENRY. Oh, she knows that's hopeless. (*Drinks.*) It's the acting, I suppose. (*Pause.*) I've never understood what it's like to want something so much that you go downhill if you don't get it. (*Drinks.*) I think I've been at the bottom of the hill since I was born. (*Drinks.*) They say the only way from there is upwards, but it's not true. I screwed up my career in the army through sheer inertia. (*Drinks.*) I've been lucky though. Whenever I've been on the brink of having to make an effort, something's always come along. Like Austin saying I could live here. All found. No worries. I do little jobs. (*Grins.*) I play the gentleman's gentleman a bit when I feel like it. Makes Austin furious. But then we laugh, you know. (*Drinks.*) Little games. (*Pause.*) He lives in this house like . . . a man who's given up. (*Drinks.*) I suppose we both do. (*Drinks.*) Well what is there, anyway? (*Standing.*) Come on. It's time you were introduced in the Fox. The pub, you know.

VALODYA. They have Russian vodka?

HENRY. Well. Polish, anyway.

VALODYA. Ah, the Poles! (*Lifts his glass.*) Nazdrowie! (*Drinks.*) The Irish of Central Europe.

HENRY. By God they were magnificent bastards in the war —

Pause.

VALODYA. They still are, Henry.

Pause.

HENRY. I don't think Glenda's got your measure at all.

VALODYA. You are charitable.

HENRY. If things got bad here, I mean really bad. If I had to run from England. (*Pause.*) I don't think I could face it anywhere else. (*Pause.*) I feel for anyone that has to leave their country.

Pause.

VALODYA (*drinks, grins*). No point sitting there in Leningrad waiting for White House to pick Cousin Vladimir by scruff of neck and drag him to freedom. What has he done to deserve such a thing?

HENRY. Fuck all, I should think.

VALODYA. How true. (*Pause.*) Come. We go through house. I must take a coat.

HENRY. In this weather?

Pause.

VALODYA. It comforts me.

HENRY. Right.

VALODYA *saunters towards the steps, swinging at a branch with his stick, and not omitting to fill his glass on the way.* HENRY *watches him go.*

HENRY. Are you Jewish?

VALODYA. It matters here?

HENRY. Not much since we got the Pakistanis.

VALODYA *is going up the steps. At the top he turns to look down on* HENRY.

VALODYA. I give that damn Cousin Alexei three thousand roubles to — how is it? Fiddle our exit visas. Push them on a little. And what does this criminal do? (*Pause.*) He fixes them for Israel!

HENRY. As I understand it, they don't make a habit of letting the gentiles out. Do they? Should be counting your blessings old lad.

VALODYA. Henry. I am kicked from my laboratory into Red Army. Who knows if it is malice on high or incompetence below? I fight one war from Kiev to Berlin. Miraculously, I live. And Alexei should want me murdered by the Syrians? I pay him three thousand roubles to stick my neck into Middle East problem? How's *that* for anti-semitism!

He drains his glass, tosses it into the garden and disappears into the house. HENRY *shuffles up the garden towards the steps.*

Fade out.

Scene Four

The garden. Night. There is a soft illumination from paper lanterns in the trees, and a glow from the house at the back.

AUSTIN slouches in a chair by the tape-deck, a glass in his hand. The Marlene Dietrich tape is playing again, very quietly.

KATYA is gathering bottles and glasses onto a large tray. She has changed into an attractive summer dress bought in Vienna. She looks up at the trees.

KATYA. Pretty lanterns —

AUSTIN. That was Henry's fifty-eighth birthday. (*Pause.*) No event so trivial that the Hard Core doesn't seize upon it. (*Drinks.*) Matter of fact, those Chinese lanterns went up the first time when Smidge's beagle died.

KATYA. Who's Smidge?

AUSTIN. Gordon shot it. (*Pause.*) They'll all be round, later on. (*Drinks.*) They're inevitable. (*Drinks.*) They give that word 'inevitable' its full, awesome resonance.

Pause.

KATYA. I love the heat and the stillness. I didn't expect it, in London.

AUSTIN. I wish I could remember a bit more about Vienna.

Pause.

KATYA. Are you drunk now, Austin?

AUSTIN. I don't think so. (*Pause.*) Not very. (*Pause.*) Not for me.

Pause.

KATYA. It's very peaceful here.

AUSTIN. Not for long. (*Looks at his watch.*) Nearly closing time at the pub.

KATYA. Why do you tolerate these people? (*Pause.*) And if you really want to stop drinking —

AUSTIN. I wonder if I do?

KATYA. Such people never let go. (*Smiles wanly.*) They don't like defectors.

Pause.

AUSTIN. What did you say that man's name was? The one on the plane?

KATYA. Pringle.

Pause.

AUSTIN. What booze does to the memory!

KATYA *comes to sit near him.*

KATYA. Do you remember me?

AUSTIN. Well. There you are, at any rate.

KATYA. Valodya and I can still go to Israel.

AUSTIN. How can you be so incredibly unrealistic about him? (*Drinks.*) I have one vivid flash in my mind. Valodya at the Jewish Agency in Vienna. (*Imitating* VALODYA.) 'Of course I shall require a car, and a substantial apartment in Tel Aviv — '

KATYA. He was drunk.

AUSTIN. Exactly.

KATYA. And you too.

AUSTIN. Exactly.

KATYA. He — performs.

AUSTIN. Don't we all?

KATYA. Can you imagine the shock of suddenly being here? The strangeness? (*Pause.*) Everything in Vienna seems dream-like. Meeting you. The — the marriage. Coming to London. (*Pause.*) It's been too much. I don't know what I've done. It's frightening.

AUSTIN. Just don't make me start resenting what *I've* done.

Pause.

KATYA. This Glenda thinks I am a foolish victim of you and Valodya. A dull, passive creature. (*Standing.*) But I do want a new life. I can go my own way. (*Pause.*) I'm furious with myself now.

AUSTIN *takes his glass to the table and refills it.*

AUSTIN. Do you know what dear old Cousin Vladimir's been doing? For years, on and off?

Pause.

KATYA (*sitting*). Almost nothing. I don't ask. (*Pause.*) One should not ask.

AUSTIN. He must be the only physicist who ever got rich buying stolen knitwear right across the Soviet Republics — and selling it back to factory managers so they could meet their official quotas. (*Drinks.*) How's that for the ironies of public ownership of the means of production?

KATYA. Our whole system is a crime! So then how do we judge somebody? (*Pause.*) Are you judging?

Pause.

AUSTIN. No. I'm a bit short on moral rectitude. (*Drinks.*) I think Valodya displayed a commendable sense of humour, in the midst of the great Soviet travail.

Pause.

KATYA. I know he is cynical.

AUSTIN. Cynical? God knows there's an anti-semitic streak in the Russians, but how does he play it? He's an upright Soviet citizen when he's fiddling the stolen knitwear market, and positively rabbinical when he wants to get out. (*Pause.*) Has he shown you that discharge paper from a Moscow psychiatric hospital? Forged, of course. He's never been in one. Just thought it might come in useful. As far as I can make out, you have to be implacably sane to get in a Soviet nuthouse. He'd never make it. He's an outrage to the suffering of genuinely persecuted people in your country.

KATYA. I know he loves and respects you.

AUSTIN. Because I married you and got him through the immigration at Heathrow? (*Drinks.*) He'd better love me. Serve him right if I had him paying off that debt for the rest of his life.

KATYA. You were insensible at the airport. We were fortunate to have that Mr Pringle with us. He was very kind.

AUSTIN. No doubt. But I imagine it was handy to have our marriage certificate to wave in their faces. On the face of it your Austin Proctor's a well-heeled solid citizen, fit to act as guarantor and all the rest of it. A bit corpselike when drunk but a clean record. (*Pause.*) I wish I'd seen their faces. Don't you think as immigrants go, Vladimir's in a class all on his own? He has absolutely *no idea* how undesirable he is. (*He sees her looking at his glass.*) Will you please not count them?

KATYA (*rising*). You have no intention to stop. (*She fetches a bottle and refills his glass.*) All he wanted was to get out and live somewhere in peace. (*As he grabs the bottle and adds more.*) He's not well.

AUSTIN. His liver, I should think. He drinks more than I do.

KATYA. And carries it better.

AUSTIN. I should throw you both out.

KATYA. It won't be necessary.

AUSTIN. Not well! That man intends to have a ball before something terminal carries him off. He may look like Ivan Denisovitch, but he's about as fragile as a pig's arse. (*Drinks.*) I should stop drinking at this point in my life?

KATYA. I wish people knew why they ever started.

AUSTIN. I like it, I can afford it and so far as I know I haven't ruined anybody else's life with it. (*Pause.*) Could we say that about work, for example?

KATYA. So long as you ruin only yourself —

AUSTIN. *Am* I a ruin?

KATYA (*sitting*). In Vienna you said you needed someone to be sober for. (*A thin smile.*) A likely story.

AUSTIN. It's true I do sometimes get maudlin when I've had a few.

Pause.

KATYA. Did you tell me anything true in Vienna at all?

AUSTIN. I doubt it. (*Pause.*) They definitely weren't training fourteen-year-olds for Spitfire pilots in nineteen-forty. (*Drinks.*) As for my role in the assassination of Heidrich, I think I was in the fifth form at the time. (*Drinks.*) My father wasn't killed in the Spanish Civil War. Three weeks after he won a fortune on the football pools two years ago, he and my mother were found dead in a hotel in Paris. (*Pause.*) I should imagine they had their hands locked round each other's throats. My mother was an Agatha Christie fan. Her idea of the spree of a lifetime was a trip on the Orient Express. (*Drinks.*) I inherited two hundred and eleven thousand pounds less the price of two return tickets from Paris to

Istanbul. (*Drinks.*) So now you know the ridiculous origins of my bank balance.

KATYA (*rising*) Let's go in. Austin.

AUSTIN. The last paper Valodya published was brilliant. (*Pause.*) The omega-minus particle. Nineteen sixty-three. (*Pause.*) It was the dim, drunken memory of a fine scientist that took me to Vienna. I was intrigued. I wondered how a man who'd never criticised or opposed the authorities had got himself excommunicated. (*Drinks.*) I would have thought his combination of scientific brilliance and personal opportunism ideal for a glowing career in the Soviet Union. (*Drinks.*) I wish he'd picked something a bit more riveting than knitwear! (*Drinks.*) Shame on him!

Pause.

KATYA. What did you pick?

AUSTIN. I think I'll switch to vodka. (*He crosses to the table, searches among the bottles.*)

KATYA. What did you pick, Austin?

He stands measuring the vodka into a glass, very carefully and deliberately.

AUSTIN. A couple of years ago I was sitting in my lab and I had a very strange experience. I won't tax the lay brain with concepts and calculations. (*Drinks.*) At the level of inquiry I was into, the common-sense world of energy, time, space and a matter becomes — insubstantial. (*Drinks.*) A bit like walking through cobwebs in a dark room. (*Drinks.*) I suddenly had a terrible sense of vertigo. An endless falling sensation. (*Drinks.*) It's never quite gone away. (*Pause.*) I walked out of the lab and I've never gone back. (*Drinks.*) Nothing mysterious about it. In the last thirty years I've met two other physicists who confessed to a similar experience. It isn't religious, or metaphysical. You're just — appalled. You either shake it off and go on, or it stays and you're — fucked, as it were. (*Drinks.*) At least, inheriting nearly two hundred thousand quid makes the sensation almost luxurious. I thrive on it, in my perverse way.

Pause.

KATYA. Was it anything to do with how your work could be used?

AUSTIN. Christ no! I've never been haunted by that one. (*Drinks.*) That's the Frankenstein fallacy. Strictly for Hollywood or any other breed of romanticism.

KATYA. Such as Mary Shelley's?

Pause.

AUSTIN. Katya. I was stewing in my own juice very nicely, thank you very much. Till all this. (*Pause.*) Henry and I were going to just quietly sit things out, you know. Set in our ways. No fuss. No complaints. Lofty observers of the democratic tragedy and all that. (*Pause.*) If you and Vladimir don't leave, it's all right by me. But don't count on me for anything, d'you see?

Pause.

KATYA (*moving away*). Good night, then —

AUSTIN. Do you seriously think I'm going to spare you the tedium of meeting the Hard Core?

KATYA. I don't wish it.

He crosses to her unsteadily.

AUSTIN. I tell you what, Katya. I'll just drink for a day or two. (*Cooing.*) Coming down eeeever so gently. Then we'll sort things out. Eh?

KATYA. Not if those people are going to be in and out all the time.

Pause.

AUSTIN. Then bugger off to Tel Aviv.

He sits down heavily, hugging the bottle to his chest. KATYA *starts walking away up the garden.*

AUSTIN. And take Cousin bloody Vladimir with you!

KATYA *turns and comes back towards him.*

KATYA. I suppose you practically grew up knowing the facts about the Soviet Union!

AUSTIN. That's right.

KATYA. As understood in the West.

Pause.

AUSTIN. Don't let's have that conversation. Not you and me Katya. I've endured it so many times at scientific conferences. Paris. Geneva. New York. My eyes glaze over and I go stiff with boredom.

Pause.

KATYA. It's very strange to look at you and know that what was a terrible revelation to me is something you've taken for granted about my country all your life.

AUSTIN. Yes. It must be humiliating.

KATYA. Why should you mock me? I don't think anyone here could begin to understand the degree of anger and humiliation. (*Pause.*) It is possible to live one's life there and not to realise. If you've been brought up that way, and educated that way. (*Pause.*) I was into my thirties before I questioned a single thing. I went to the Institute every day and taught English nineteenth-century literature. I did my own research —

AUSTIN. And heard whispers? And rumours? And ignored them?

KATYA. Yes!

AUSTIN. And had access to Western papers and thought them full of lies?

KATYA (*shouting*). Up to a point!

AUSTIN. What point?

Pause.

KATYA. I lived quietly. I did my work. I had my friends. (*Pause.*) I fell in love, and married. My husband was a librarian, with a passion for mediaeval history. We were very happy for eight years. He died of leukaemia. (*Pause.*) I started a book on the Brontës and became rather solitary. Apart from Sasha, I'd never felt very close to anyone. (*Pause.*) A blue-stocking, is it? (*Pause.*) You can be educated and intelligent, and still unaware of a great deal. Certainly in Russia. What Valodya calls a 'controlled environment'. (*Pause.*) Some years ago he knocked on my door late one night and asked if he could stay till the morning. I hadn't seen him since before my marriage. (*Pause.*) I only had one room. He slept on the couch. (*Pause.*) Months later he came again. Then quite regularly. (*Pause.*) You talk about being appalled by that experience in your laboratory. He said he was appalled by me. (*Pause.*) Ignorant. Naïve. Conformist. (*Pause.*) I liked him but he frightened me somehow. He used to laugh, and drink a lot. He said he was re-educating me. My first shock was when he said he preferred the failed American dream to the successful Russian nightmare. (*She smiles.*) Then *I* was appalled. (*Pause.*) I realise nothing of what he told me is news to a thinking person in the West. Or for that matter a handful of people in my own country. (*Pause.*) As for the ignorant over here, it's sad they pick it up as little more than a casual prejudice. (*Pause.*) Valodya woke me up. It reminded me of when I was told I had to start wearing glasses at the age of thirteen. I hadn't realised I was actually short-sighted. (*Pause.*) Quite a transformation. (*Pause.*) My mother was Jewish. It was never made much of, one way or the other, in our family. (*Pause.*) I began to think of trying to get out, though. And Valodya encouraged me.

AUSTIN. The sly bastard!

KATYA. *No!*

AUSTIN. Oh, come on, Katya – he was planning against the day they caught up with him, wasn't he?

KATYA. That is ridiculous and insulting.

Pause.

AUSTIN. And what would you say about your predicament at the moment?

The garden gate bursts open, and the Hard Core comes staggering through – cheerfully drunk, laughing, singing 'Here comes the bride'. They stumble in a circle round AUSTIN *and* KATYA *bawling at the tops of their voices.* SMIDGE *has a paper bag from which she scatters confetti over* AUSTIN, *who sits grinning foolishly. As they subside:*

AUSTIN. That's Annie, Smidge, Len, Glenda . . . you've met Glenda. (*He stands swaying and thumps* GORDON *on the shoulder.*) And this is good old Gordon. Backbone of the recession.

KATYA. We were just going in.

The Hard Core regards her with disbelief. HENRY *is already doling out drinks.*

AUSTIN. The wretched woman's drink-shy, d'you see –

GORDON. Absolutely forbidden, verboten and interdit. (*He dumps a carrier on the table, takes out three wine bottles and waves them in front of* KATYA.) What'll the good lady have? We have Reisling, Hock and Bol-hock —

KATYA. Nothing, thank you.

GORDON. I didn't hear that. (*Grabs a drink from* HENRY.) Cheers. (*Pats her cheek and turns away.*) I don't know about you, friends. But after that session in the pub I'm as parched as a fart up the arsehole of a curried duck.

SMIDGE. It isn't every day of the week we get married. Is it dear?

GORDON. Pick that bloody confetti up, Smidge. It's not your lawn —

SMIDGE *sinks to her knees, picking at the confetti.*

GORDON. I tell you. If I led her up the Post Office tower and said 'jump off', she'd do it. She'd have to. She has this restless urge to obey me.

SMIDGE (*dottily crooning*). There's rosemary, that's for remembrance.

GORDON. Marvellous. She did *Much Ado About Nothing* for her School Certificate in nineteen forty-four, and it's the only thing that's stuck in her head ever since.

SMIDGE. And there is pansies. That's for thoughts —

GLENDA. Till that her garments, heavy with their drink/Pulled the poor wretch from her melodious lay/To muddy death —

GORDON. One thing old Smidge is *not* is a melodious lay.

ANNIE (*leaning heavily on* KATYA). I 'ope you aren't goin' to turn out a spoilsport, darlin' —

LEN. Where's Ivan the Terrible? Have we lost him? (*Drinks.*) Tried to fill me with some crap in the pub. Says they don't need private detectives in Russia. Says I'd be nationalised if it happened here. (*Pause.*) I'm not as fucking dim as I look, I told him. My blank-faced anonymity is part of the appearance required by the job. (*Drinks.*) The Russian theory, he said, is that if nine people out of ten are innocent — they can't be.

SMIDGE. I think he's having a pee in your rhododendron tubs in the front, Austin —

LEN. One of those remarks that rings true but you can't work out why.

We hear VALODYA *loudly singing a Russian song. He appears in the glass doors and declaims from the platform:*

VALODYA. Friends. comrades, parteignossen —

LEN. And what if he's a spy?

VALODYA *rattles down the steps in slow motion, gathering himself into an elegant pose on the lawn and taking the glass proffered instanta by* HENRY. *He points his stick at the sky, bending one knee slightly.*

VALODYA. I look at velvet sky. At burning stars. (*Sips.*) And decide universe is not convincing. (*Pause.*) Boga niet!

ANNIE. Wha's that?

KATYA. There is no God.

HENRY. Christ almighty!

VALODYA. Free *press* is mighty, Henry. (*Waves a paper.*) I read one of your kremlinologists in lavatory. How nice to be an expert on Russian affairs. And every time you open your mouth some newspaper puts a cheque in it. (*Tossing the paper aside.*) Will they pay Valodya? I have not two roubles to rub together.

ANNIE (*to* KATYA, *moving off*). *Try* to enjoy yourself darlin'. (*Pulls* LEN *to the tape-deck.*) Come and dance with little Annie —

They fumble with the cassettes and eventually produce some Glen Miller. AUSTIN *has been standing all this time with his eyes closed, like a machine switched off except for the purpose of raising his glass.* GORDON *prods him in the ribs.*

GORDON. Austin? (*Pause.*) Austin? (*Pause: to* KATYA.) That's how he goes sometimes. (*Pause.*) Austin? Yes he's gone. It's his normal way. Don't panic. Best thing is just to sit him down. (*Pulls a chair forward and pushes* AUSTIN *into it.*) Just ignore him. (*Drinks.*) It'll take you a year or two to get used to his little ways.

He wanders off. KATYA *kneels beside* AUSTIN *and gently removes the glass from his fingers.* VALODYA *and* HENRY *are precariously seated at the chess table.*

HENRY (*leaning forward confidentially, chin misses cupped hand*). You were saying about Einstein?

VALODYA. Is very simple, Henry. Theory is that when body is travelling at speed of light in vacuum — has infinite mass. OK? (HENRY *nods sagely.*) Now. You might ask: what is infinite mass, old chap?

HENRY. What *is* infinite mass?

> HENRY *sways dangerously and* VALODYA *restores him upright with exaggerated care. They grin foolishly at one another and raise their glasses.* GLENDA *has found herself a place under a tree and is pretending an aloof disinterest.* ANNIE *and* LEN *sway in a clumsy embrace without moving.* SMIDGE *sits by herself drinking and counting pieces of confetti from one hand to the other.* GORDON *looms over* KATYA *again.*

GORDON (*drinks*). A few words of advice. I take it you speak our lingo? Don't try to put the ring through his nose, sweetheart. (*Drinks.*) You'll need friends. We're his friends. Ergo we are your friends — eh? (*Pats her cheek.*) That's my girl —

> KATYA *steps back, staring at him. He bends genially over* AUSTIN.

GORDON. Communism! (*Lifting one of* AUSTIN's *eyelids.*) Used to be quite leftish meself, you know. We've all been young and fiery. In our time. (*Lifting the other.*) He's all right. Asleep, that's all (*Drinks.*) Great fighters, the Russians. (*Drinks.*) Daft to talk about it so many years afterwards, I suppose. Incredible how many people in this country still do. Old lags. Out of touch. Bar-fly bores, you know. Time they all died off. (*Drinks.*) Tanks, meself. The desert. Italy. Normandy. The Rhine. (*Smiling.*) Champagne all the way. (*Drinks.*) Knocked out twice. Damn lucky to be alive. Insofar as we all are alive. (*Drinks.*) Awful bugger Stalin must have been. Old Uncle Joe —

> *Pause.*

KATYA. Stalin has been dead for twenty-five years.

GORDON. Has he really? (*Singing and hopping.*) And it don't seem a day too much —

KATYA (*loudly and fiercely*). I wish you would all get out of here.

GLENDA. Whoops!

GORDON. Now just a minute —

KATYA (*pointing at* AUSTIN). Look at this man!

> GORDON *takes* AUSTIN's *head between his hands. He pulls it forward, then lets it sag back.*

GORDON. It's a free world, ducky. (*Drinks.*) On our side of the iron curtain.

> *He jabs* AUSTIN's *shoulder and proffers his glass. Eyes closed,* AUSTIN *automatically reaches out and takes it. Drinks.*

GORDON. Still. Doesn't seem to matter who's on top over there. Does it? Gangsters one and all —

KATYA. Does it matter over here?

> *She goes into the house.* HENRY *staggers after her but nearly falls. He grabs a tree branch and hangs there.*

GORDON. I mean you can tell me straight out, Henry. You're second in command here, old bumface. (*Drinks.*) I mean if we're unwelcome guests in Austin's own house —

HENRY (*pointing at* SMIDGE). It was Hamlet she was quoting from. Not Mushadooaboutnothing —

GORDON. Eh?

HENRY. You ask Glenda. (*Goes to bend over* AUSTIN, *leans on his shoulders.*) Alas poor Yorick! (*Pulls* AUSTIN's *head forward by the hair.*) A fellow of infinite mass —

GORDON (*looking at* VALODYA). If she thinks the Hard Core's going to take this lying down —

VALODYA. I wish only to drink and look at stars. (*Drinks.*) Beautiful stars of social democracy. (*Drinks.*) Twinkling.

> HENRY *heads for the house but can't coordinate, and turns back.*

HENRY. What about me? (*Belches.*) I get the impression somebody's days are numbered.

GORDON. It won't be yours, sonny boy.

> SMIDGE *has been pulling herself upright by her tree. She stands with her face pressed to the bark.*

SMIDGE (*bursting into tears*). I feel sorry for her!

GORDON. Women!

SMIDGE. That's right. Go on. Yes. It's women, isn't it —

GORDON. Yes it's all you God-forsaken cows.

SMIDGE (*wailing*). I drink because you do, Gordon.

GORDON (*snaps his fingers*). Come!

She comes cringing towards him. He puts an arm round her shoulders and holds his glass to her lips. As she drinks:

GORDON. Now why does she drink?

SMIDGE (*ingratiatingly*). Because she likes it?

GORDON. We can do better than that. Let's start again shall we?

SMIDGE. Because she's ugly? (*Drinks.*) And middle-aged? (*Drinks.*) And stupid an' gaga?

GORDON (*snaps his fingers*). Yes?

SMIDGE. Because she can't run Gordon's office?

GLENDA. Stop it, Gordon!

He pushes SMIDGE away and crosses to GLENDA.

GORDON. Glenda likes her drinkey-winkey too, Smidge. Glenda sees cracks in the walls, with nasty things coming out. (*Pause.*) Henry likes it. Austin likes it. (*He looks at ANNIE, who is asleep with her head cradled in LEN's lap.*) Annie and Len like it. (*At VALODYA.*) What's-his-name likes it —

GLENDA *leads* SMIDGE *sobbing up the garden into the house. As they go:*

GORDON (*shouting*). But Smidgey can't fucking well live without it! (*Turns on HENRY, smiling garishly.*) Not with wit, decency or poise —

Pause.

HENRY. Cut it out, Gordon.

GORDON. But did you ever see anything more pathetic? And it's probably pissed itself again, as it so often does when boozed. It won't be the first time Glenda's changed her.

He fills his glass, shouting at the house.

GORDON. I only have to look at her. Sodden. Trembling. Whining. (*Drinks.*) And I grow eloquent from sheer revulsion.

(*Slumping visibly: to* VALODYA.) Let me tell you, my shady
foreign friend. If I had two hundred thousand pounds — I'd
have dumped her long ago. (*He crosses to* ANNIE *and stirs
with his foot.*) But what does one do, my dear old Bolshevik
mate? (ANNIE *slips sideways onto the grass in a stupor.*) If
one is — let's face it — unprincipled, mediocre, and mildly
corrupt?

VALODYA. One emigrates.

GORDON (*laughing, he grabs* VALODYA's *shoulder*). I think
we ought to drag him to Johnny's Bar. Don't you Henry?
(*Drinks.*) The night is young. (*The three of them stare at*
AUSTIN.) It wouldn't do our patron saint any harm, either.

HENRY. I'm scared stiff of his wife. (*Drinks.*) Can it be that
twenty-four hours ago I was screaming with boredom? What
bliss! (*Pause.*) I feel hideously sober all of a sudden.

GORDON. Soon put you out of your misery. Come on —

HENRY. What about Smidge? You really are the most awful
prick, Gordon.

GORDON. I know. (*To* VALODYA.) You coming? I feel like
painting the town *red?*

Pause.

VALODYA. I think I will stay.

GORDON. Suit yourself —

*They go out through the garden gate. It is very quiet.
Somewhere at a party a record starts up. The sound comes
and goes faintly, on a light breeze. ANNIE lifts her head, croaking.*

ANNIE. Gi' me a drink, somebody —

*VALODYA goes to the table and pours water into a glass.
He takes it to her.*

ANNIE. Ain't nothing wrong with me that divorcin' that
bastard husband of mine couldn't cure. (*Pause.*) If it wasn't
for my little girl, I'd — (*Sips.*) Water! You bleedin' maniac —

*She throws the glass down and passes out again. VALODYA
sits at the chess table and lines up the pieces. AUSTIN opens
his eyes and leans forward.*

AUSTIN. Boo!

Pause.

VALODYA. Henry and Gordon have gone to Johnny's Bar.

AUSTIN. I heard.

VALODYA. I think you heard all. (*Pause.*) And you do nothing.

AUSTIN. I did what you've been doing all your life, Valodya.

VALODYA (*wearily*). That is childish. (*He gestures at the garden.*) And look what your life has come to. (*Drinks.*) Fools, failures and parasites.

AUSTIN *goes to the table for a drink.* VALODYA's *paper lies nearby. As he pours, he kicks at it.*

AUSTIN. So you read the latest bit of kremlinology, did you? (*He gulps the drinks and pours another, picks up the paper.*) Apart from the Grigorenkos and Ginsburgs. The Bukhovskys and Sakharovs. The what shall we call them? The moral giants?

VALODYA. Please, Austin —

AUSTIN *finds the place he is looking for and reads out. A liturgy.*

AUSTIN. Bogatyrev: died of a broken skull. Attacked by persons unknown outside his house in Moscow. (*Pause.*) Victor Shalamberidze: he and family killed in a mysterious car crash. (*Pause.*) Dmitry Dudko: interrogated and threatened by the K.G.B. Legs broken in a subsequent car crash. (*Pause.*) Kryuchov: beaten and tortured in his flat by unknown assailants. (*Pause.*) Bershtam: beaten up by four men who said they would kill him if he didn't leave for Israel. Nikolai Zhuk: another broken skull. Reported now in a psychiatric clinic. (*He crosses to* VALODYA *and raises his glass.*) Whereas. Vladimir Konstantin Rusakov: physicist. Reluctant soldier. Deserter. Imprisoned. Amnestied. Successful black marketeer. (*Drinks.*) If I thought there were mitigating circumstances, I might sober up just to hear them. (*Drinks.*) Why *did* I bring the Russian cuckoo into my little nest! (*He moves away.*) Why didn't I just tell you to piss off, in Vienna?

Pause.

VALODYA (*rising*). I should think. Whatever you may say. (*Pause.*) However drunk you were. (*Pause.*) You wanted Katya.

AUSTIN. The extraordinary thing is, Valodya, I regard myself as a man devoid of any moral convictions whatsoever — and yet the very sight of you enrages me. (*Drinks.*) I can hear a shrill, self-righteous tone in my voice when I speak to you. Or about you. (*Drinks.*) Granted, only when the tide of booze recedes a little. None the less. You make me feel irritable, and cheated. You make me feel sullen, mean-spirited. Make me want to kick things, piss on flowers, insult the nearest cripple. (*Drinks.*) Now why is that? Why *do* you have this ridiculous effect on me? (*Drinks.*) I think I'm ashamed of you. It's most annoying. I wish you'd never left Leningrad. You're a nuisance. A problem. I really don't think I want to take you on.

Pause.

VALODYA. And Katya?

AUSTIN. Why don't the pair of you just stick a pin in a map? How about Australia? That's a nice long way away. (*Drinks.*) America? *(Drinks.)* I suppose in the knitwear business you didn't have much time to keep up with theoretical physics? (*Pause.*) What *do* sleazy Russian exiles do? If you have neither a useful profession nor moral authority in life's great ideological conflict, what on earth use are you to anybody? (*Puts his glass down and heads for the gate.*) I'm off to drown my sorrows —

ANNIE *stirs, props herself up on her elbow looking from* AUSTIN *to* VALODYA.

AUSTIN (*at the gate*). Coming?

Pause.

VALODYA. Why not?

ANNIE. Welcome to the 'Ard Core, darlin' —

She slumps out cold again. AUSTIN *goes out.* VALODYA *stands over* ANNIE *and* LEN. *He takes one of the rugs from the lawn and carefully spreads it over them. He goes.*

End of Part One.

PART TWO

The sitting room of AUSTIN PROCTOR's *house. A very large, high-ceilinged room with tall window-doors set in a deep, wide alcove overlooking the garden. A door to the hall. The room is light, modern and colourful: large modern paintings, sofas and chairs in leather and rough-textured material in autumn colours, dark blues and greens. There are cushions, rugs, low tables, books and magazines scattered about. In one corner there is a table crowded with bottles, glasses, tonics etc. In another, a hi-fi, record shelves, etc. A long table stands in the alcove, covered with a white damask cloth. On it there are piles of gleaming cutlery and plates, glasses, cups and saucers, bowls of flowers.*

Scene Five

Late morning, the day after AUSTIN's *homecoming. The heavy curtains on the big window are drawn back, and sunshine pours into the room.*

   HENRY *enters in an orange towelling bathrobe and blue canvas shoes with rope soles. He is carrying a cup of coffee which rattles loudly on its saucer. He stands by the fireplace trying to drink it. His hands shake so badly that he finally sets the cup on a table and kneels to drink. He burns his lips, and crouches back on his heels staring at the cup malevolently.*

   AUSTIN *enters, also with a cup of coffee. He looks surprisingly fresh: shaved, clean white shirt, black trousers and casual shoes.*

HENRY. Morning, Austin.

AUSTIN. You awful little bastard.

   AUSTIN *tries to drink his coffee.* HENRY *gleefully watches him trying to cope with a similar shakes problem to his own.* AUSTIN *crosses to the big table and stares at the preparations.*

AUSTIN. What's all this?

HENRY. Search me.

AUSTIN (*turning*). Let me put it this way, Henry —

HENRY. State your problem, and thy will be done, master.

AUSTIN. Top bathroom: Len stone cold in the bath. Top front bedroom: Gordon and Annie. Top back: Glenda in a sea of puke. (*Pause.*) So-called 'utility room': Smidge in a coma with her head in a plastic basin. And when we take our tom-tom headache for a brisk shower, Henry — what is the state of the first floor bathroom?

HENRY. Haven't been in. No urge to pee this morning. I don't know why not. Constriction, you know. Bottleneck. Tight as a cat's bum. Hope it's not the prostate.

AUSTIN. A smashed bag of crisps, two empty bottles, a broken glass and a wine-soddened copy of *The Gulag Archipelago*.

Pause.

HENRY. It all sounds perfectly normal to me. Don't you remember last night?

AUSTIN. Of course I don't bloody remember.

Pause.

HENRY. Neither do I. (*Pause.*) How's your wife?

AUSTIN. My arrangement, Henry.

HENRY. Your arrangement.

AUSTIN. If she has any sense, she'll be down at London Airport booked on the first plane to Tel Aviv.

HENRY. You don't — sleep together?

AUSTIN. That wasn't included in the terms.

HENRY. What a shame.

AUSTIN. It might be, if I were a small grey fuck-starved shit like you Henry. (*He crosses to the drinks and absently pours two.*) I don't want sex, I want oblivion. (*Takes one to HENRY.*) Here. Start the day as we mean to go on. (*They drink.*) I think you'd better put me on a long chain. Don't you *ever* let me take off abroad again when I'm on a bender.

HENRY. What can I do if you disappear in the middle of the night?

AUSTIN. Well to start with, what about having shackles fitted to my bed? I'm a danger to everything that lives and moves.

I'm a lunatic. Go and write it on that memory slate of yours in the kitchen: bed shackles for Austin. Handcuffs. Strait-jacket. The lot. (*Sitting, he looks round the room.*) God. Sometimes I look at this house and I see 'win', 'draw' or 'away' stamped on every bloody inch of it. (*Drinks.*) I can just see my mother and father in that hotel room in Paris. Her nagging for Istanbul and him whining for Worthing. (*He presses his hands together, raising his eyes to the ceiling.*) Dear mother and father: I have abandoned thermo-nuclear fusion in order to spend your money on everything you'd disapprove of.

HENRY. Makes you think though, doesn't it?

AUSTIN. Absolutely nothing makes me think these days, Henry.

HENRY. I mean — what have we to complain about compared with those poor buggers in Russia? (*Drinks.*) According to Valodya —

AUSTIN. *Do* I complain?

HENRY. You don't, actually. Come to think of it. (*Pause.*) I have a dim recollection of him dancing the gopak last night at Johnny's. (*Slaps his thigh.*) It's his birthday today! That's what that's all about — another celebration, old lad.

AUSTIN. The fact that he's still alive is something to celebrate?

HENRY. Oh come on. Make the best of it. (*Drinks.*) For Katya's sake anyway. (*Pause.*) I had the impression she cares about you.

AUSTIN. Like most of your impressions, Henry, it's just one more symptom of your pathetic addiction to insecurity.

HENRY *wanders disconsolately to the window and looks out.*

HENRY. Will they be staying? (*Pause.*) Do you want me out?

AUSTIN. No. So do me a favour and go up and disperse the Hard Core, will you?

HENRY. It's pretty bleak out there on one's own. At my age.

AUSTIN. The very same thought crossed my mind when I was in my pram.

GLENDA *comes in, heading straight for the drinks.*

GLENDA (*passing AUSTIN*). It's all right. I've cleaned it all up. Including me. (*Touching a bottle.*) Eeny meeny miny mo —

a little drink and then I'll go. (*Pours one.*) I should have been at an audition yesterday afternoon. But I wasn't, was I? (*Raising her glass.*) Here's to burning ambition.

KATYA *comes in with a huge bag of groceries in her arms. She looks excited and very attractive.*

KATYA. Austin, I — oh, I'm sorry.

AUSTIN. What for? Do I know you?

HENRY *has pushed his glass behind his back.* GLENDA *ostentatiously pours herself another and fills* AUSTIN's *glass.*

KATYA. I was going to explain —

AUSTIN. Explain what? The festive board over there? I see you've found Henry's grandma's silver. And Mrs Proctor's Crown Derby from Harrods. But why bother to explain, when you already feel so free? Why not just use the place like everybody else does?

GORDON. Coffee, coffee, coffee —

He comes in and collapses at once on a couch, with his hands over his eyes.

GORDON. Oh God. Oh Jesus. Pray walk on tiptoe, all ye who come near Gordon.

KATYA (*putting the bag down*). I'll get him some —

GORDON. Don't worry. I've got Smidge on to it. If she doesn't get her tits caught in the grinder.

KATYA. Are you all drinking already?

GORDON. What a bloody good idea. (*Going to the drinks.*) Got to get in shape, haven't we? (*Raising his glass.*) The first of the day keeps the doctor away —

GLENDA (*to* KATYA). The routine is, lovey - - we all gather round the morning after, and nurse each other till we've got the strength to make it to the Fox. (*Drinks.*) It may seem ghastly to you but it's vital to us. Otherwise we're not fit to drink with.

KATYA. Were you fit yesterday?

GLENDA. Yesterday is an awesome blank, darling. (*Drinks.*) Yesterday does not exist. Ask Austin. Yesterday was a hole in the head even the morning after the night he had me. *Not* very long ago. Was it, my love?

She sprawls in a chair with her glass, smiling. SMIDGE *comes in carrying a tray with coffee. In the silence, the sound of the rattling cups and saucers is deafening.*

SMIDGE (*brightly*). Good morning, everybody. (*She sets the tray down beside* GORDON.) Here we are, dear.

GORDON. A bloody mug, I said.

SMIDGE. I'm sorry, Gordon —

She makes to go for the mug, but KATYA *restrains her.*

KATYA. I'll get it — (*Exits.*)

SMIDGE. I couldn't find —

GORDON. You ought to damn well know your way round Austin's kitchen by now.

AUSTIN (*crossing to* GLENDA). Did I have you? I know I had somebody. (*Looking round.*) One of you. (*Drinks.*) I've been racking my brains to think who it was. (*Pause.*) We'll just have to conclude it wasn't a memorable experience.

GLENDA. Don't play silly buggers, Austin.

He goes out.

HENRY (*quietly*). I think it's time you were on your way, Glenda.

GLENDA (*suddenly hysterical*). I can't face that shitty basement. (*Looking round.*) What's the matter with you all? You've been watching me kill myself for months! (*Screaming.*) I can't face my shitty life! I need a doctor. I need a vitamin B shot. I need some fucking valium —

She reaches to the glass doors and out into the garden, as KATYA *enters with a mug.*

GORDON. Go after her, Smidge —

For him, the tone is not unkind. SMIDGE *follows* GLENDA. KATYA *pours* GORDON's *coffee.*

GORDON. She's better off in the garden. Smidge'll calm her down. (*Drinks his coffee.*) It isn't the first time she'll have coaxed Glenda through the morning terrors. (*A long look at* KATYA.) There's a lot you shouldn't take too seriously, Mrs Proctor. (*Smiling.*) Katya.

Pause.

KATYA. I was very tired and nervous yesterday.

GORDON. I'm sure you were.

KATYA. I was going to make —

AUSTIN *enters, supporting an ashen* LEN.

KATYA (*quickly*). I was going to make a Russian meal for Valody's birthday and invite you all this afternoon.

AUSTIN *sits* LEN *down and pours him a coffee.*

GORDON. I'm sure we'd all appreciate it. Wouldn't we, Austin?

AUSTIN. I've been wondering when you'd all start eating here as well.

GORDON. If words were turds, Austin. (*To* LEN.) He'd? Come on, Len. He'd —

LEN and GORDON. He'd be a shithouse!

Pause.

AUSTIN. I wonder what delicacy of feeling prevents Annie joining us?

LEN. She's gone home.

GORDON. Oh yes?

LEN. I should think her bloke'll half kill her.

AUSTIN. Or the child.

Pause.

GORDON. You're right there. It's the kid she ought to think about. Not that I'm one to moralise. (*Drinks.*) She did make one record you know. I think I'm the only one that's been privileged. (*Drinks.*) Nineteen fifty-three. Sounds like a bull terrier with a door jammed on its neck. (*Crosses to the window and looks out.*) Sobbing on each other's shoulders down there. All nice and cosy.

LEN. Well. I'll have to be off. Quite a night, wasn't it? Thanks for the coffee.

GORDON. Courtesy of Smidge.

LEN. Quite a night wasn't it, Gordon?

GORDON. Why don't you piss off to Lords and find your client's wife? (*Turning away.*) It's going to be nice and hot again.

LEN. You see where Gordon keeps the knife, Mrs Proctor? Right between the ribs of those who've carried him home stiff with drink and tucked him into bed. Times without number. (*Pause.*) I got nicked for driving him home one night last year. Lost me licence. (*Stands up and puts his hand out to* KATYA.) We're not so bad though when you get to know us. (*Giggles.*) I couldn't tell the clutch from the brake pedal that night. And me on the side of the law, as you might say —

GORDON. You driving smack through a fence and into Regent's Park boating lake, as you might say.

LEN. I'll just say cheerio to Smidge and Glenda — (*Brushing past* GORDON.) Annie said she'll see you in the Fox at one thirty.

GORDON *raises a threatening fist, and* LEN *scuttles out.*

GORDON (*looking out*). Would you believe it, those damned women are raiding your rustic fridge, Austin? I'd better go down and break it up. (*Exits.*)

HENRY *crosses to the window and looks out.*

HENRY. Looks like the beginnings of a party already. (*Turning.*) That's Gordon's idea of breaking it up.

KATYA *takes the bag of groceries and goes out.*

HENRY. You could at least treat her in a civilised manner.

AUSTIN. Whose side are you on?

Pause.

HENRY. I'm neutral. (*Turns back to the window.*)

AUSTIN. With so much to lose?

HENRY. I've nothing more to lose. Do you think it matters to me which way I go downhill? (*Drinks.*) Makes no difference to me whether I'm skidding on your money or a pile of dogshit. (*Drinks.*) I'm ten years further down the line than you, Austin. (*Pause.*) You should go back to work. Dry out. Get off your backside. (*Gestures at the window.*) Get rid of this lot. Show 'em the door. (*Pause: shouts.*) Austin, I don't know why you've given up — do you?

Pause.

AUSTIN. Yes. I do. (*Drinks.*) So Glenda's on the verge of the D.T.'s. Smidge is dotty. Gordon's broke. Old Bob — ah, praises be! — collected his well-earned coronary last month.

And is now presumably sucking at the great whisky bottle in the sky. Ella's at the funny-farm in Harrow, so aptly named in her case. Dear George run over whilst crossing the road outside the Fox on his hands and knees. (*Drinks.*) I feel an affinity with them all, Henry. Sodden, mindless, lying, sponging, inadvertently comical — I'd rather subsidise their stubborn refusal to be tractable citizens than solve the problem of controlled fusion. (*Drinks.*) *Much* more amusing than quantum physics, I can tell you. I find their response to life quite rational.

HENRY. And I find yours tragic.

AUSTIN. I'm no loss to science. It's not like being some kind of artist. If Rutherford hadn't split the atom, somebody else would. We're hardly tempted to think the same way about Leonardo. Scientists are allowed to be eccentric, but only artists are allowed to be tormented. Whimpering and posturing and agonising. (*Drinks.*) Can you imagine trying to get a fuck at a party by announcing to the girl that you'd postulated the double helix? (*Drinks.*) If you were a controversial Hamlet, on the other hand —

HENRY. Austin, *I* heard you're something of a genius.

Pause.

AUSTIN. Now where would *you* hear *that?*

HENRY. I mean, are we to assume you've quit science in a fit of sexual pique then?

AUSTIN. Been free-loading at the Athenaeum again, have you? Lunching with that seedy Whitehall brigadier of yours?

HENRY. Dolly Sandford's a very decent man and he's on the grapevine.

AUSTIN. I hope it throttles him.

Pause.

HENRY. I blew my career in the army, Austin. (*Drinks.*) You're wasting yourself.

AUSTIN. Would you kindly go upstairs and get out of that disgusting bathrobe? You look like a balding little tart. (*As* HENRY *stalks out.*) And put some knickers on.

AUSTIN *fills his glass and crosses to the window. We hear a sudden burst of laughter from outside, and* SMIDGE's *gaga braying.* VALODYA *enters.*

AUSTIN. Your little friends are in the garden. Tearing flowers to bits and ripping the wings off butterflies.

VALODYA *gets himself a drink and crosses to the window.*

VALODYA. I bought frozen sheep.

AUSTIN. Mutton, we say. Leg of mutton. Or shoulder of lamb. Chops. That sort of thing.

VALODYA. I mean half of sheep. Of whole animal.

AUSTIN. With roubles?

VALODYA. Dollars.

AUSTIN. What *is* all this nonsense about your birthday?

VALODYA. Is not really for my birthday, Austin. Katya and I have decided to leave tomorrow. We wish to express our thanks to you. So. A little banquet for you and Henry and the Hard Core. (*Pause.*) A gesture. (*Drinks.*) So regrettable I did not arrive to England in a blaze of glory.

AUSTIN. That has nothing to do with it.

VALODYA. Still. *I* cannot play exiled voice of the Russian Conscience.

AUSTIN. No. You could hardly do that.

Pause.

VALODYA. I am sorry Katya has been hurt. (*Turning to* AUSTIN.) Insulted even. (*Holds up his hand.*) Of course I don't mean the marriage. It is not that which upsets her. (*Drinks.*) She thinks you have contempt for her.

Pause.

AUSTIN. Can you imagine how Henry and I live, Valodya?

VALODYA. Is very clear, my friend. (*Pause.*) This beautiful house reeks of more than drink. (*Drinks.*) Dulled wits. Apathy. Self-pity. (*Pause.*) Hard Core entertaining but not exactly a vigorous alternative to a life of confidence and purpose. No wives, divorces, children, maddening relatives, illnesses, deaths, bankruptcies. What on earth are you doing with yourself for half a century? Just watching?

AUSTIN. Just working.

Pause.

VALODYA. You know. We might have had the atomic bomb
ourselves during the war. That is how I came to be in the
army. (*Drinks.*) Something else I owe to Stalin. He put an end
to that line of research, and some of us found ourselves at
the front. (*Pause.*) His sense of humour. (*Drinks.*) I would
have deserted to the Americans in nineteen forty-five, but I
got ten years for disciplining my men after they burned
and looted a German village. (*Pause.*) As Lenin put it: one
step forward, two steps back.

He moves away to refill his glass and sits down.

AUSTIN. Those letters I wrote you —

VALODYA. Ah. The Soviet Union works out its wretched
destiny, Austin. But perhaps the English have uneasy
suspicion they have no destiny at all. (*Drinks.*) It must be
irritating.

AUSTIN. I think I've had some kind of nervous breakdown —

VALODYA. You're a rich man. Is much better to become a
drunk than resort to psychiatry. I have a suspicion therapy
dulls the mind.

Pause.

AUSTIN. I hate this country.

VALODYA. I hate them all.

Pause.

AUSTIN. I'm trying to say —

VALODYA. You are trying to *whine*, Austin.

AUSTIN. I can't live with my back turned.

VALODYA. We Russians have perverted a great idea and
drenched it in blood and lies. But dear me, you seem to
need our dissidents almost as badly as we do. (*Drinks.*)
How tiresome it must be to live in a country where human
rights are so respected that you must look elsewhere to
justify an otherwise futile sense of outrage.

AUSTIN. That's what I've got. That's what I'm nursing. I'm
indignant. I'm furious. If you stay in this country, have a
good look around you. Sit down and read the papers every
day, Valodya. Listen to the radio. Watch TV. Get out on the

streets. As far as I can make out, truth and liberty in our terms have a mainly masturbatory function. (*Drinks.*) Oh we do have them, yes. A human rule of law, yes. Civilised traditions. An abhorrence of the dogmatic — all stretched out tight like the skin on a boil. (*Pause.*) Beneath that skin there's a meanness, a rancour, a mindless violence brewing . . . which for the first time in three hundred years we can neither take to war nor export to some remote colony, dressed up as civilisation, honest commerce, religion or any other kind of mumbo-jumbo. (*Drinks.*) I doubt you'll ever again find so much impotent fury draining like pus into the glum business of daily existence. Or else into macabre fantasies of where to point the finger and who to smash, who to blame, how to legitimise a new order of hatred on the grounds that the old one's succumbing to violence and anarchy. (*Drinks.*) Then they want people like me to come up with controlled thermonuclear fusion as well? To provide limitless energy for the perpetuation of a society which is a rank offence to the human imagination? (*Drinks.*) Do you realise they actually want it so as to have more of what they had before? That they haven't caught on to the utter poverty of the spiritual failure so far? (*Pause.*) D'you know, a cabinet minister actually did sit in my lab mumbling about harnessing the gigantic forces of nature? He had the nerve to look me straight in the eyes. Talked of deserts flowering, turbines humming, megawatts flowing. (*Pause.*) Fuck you, old man, I said. (*Drinks.*) Fuck you. Here's my resignation. Tell whoever briefs you, I'm wildly out of touch. And take the Official Secrets Act and stuff it up your arse.

Pause.

VALODYA. My dear Austin. I had not realised you are such a puritan!

KATYA *enters, holding the door back for* PRINGLE *and* ALAN THORNTON — *tall, tanned, longish silver hair, a lightweight dark grey suit, white shirt, blue tie.* PRINGLE *is carrying a briefcase.*

THORNTON. We do hope this isn't an inconvenient moment, Proctor? At least I do. I don't think Pringle here's quite alive to the social nuance. Remember, Pringle? You were blotto yesterday I gather. Security? Bikini Atoll? (*Pause.*) Of course you were still in your nappies at Bikini. Highly privileged to be there at all, if I remember.

PRINGLE. Hello Proctor.

AUSTIN. Yesterday?

THORNTON goes to AUSTIN and puts his hand out. He has the kind of manner not easily refused. AUSTIN limply shakes hands. THORNTON goes to VALODYA and studies him.

THORNTON. And this will be Rusakov. Vladimir Konstantin. (*Puts his hand out.*) How d'you do, my dear fellow? (*Turning to KATYA.*) May I wish you all happiness, Mrs Proctor? In your new marriage. First time round for you though, Austin, isn't it?

VALODYA (*to AUSTIN*). Who is?

AUSTIN. My ex-boss. Alan Thornton.

Pause.

VALODYA. Thornton? Thornton? (*Pause.*) Conservation of parity? Was student of Wigner?

AUSTIN. The very same. But that was when *he* was his nappies. Wasn't it, Alan?

THORNTON. May we sit down? (*Pause.*) It shouldn't take very long.

He arranges himself with some care on the couch, and PRINGLE takes a chair at the back. AUSTIN stares at PRINGLE.

AUSTIN. Our man in Vienna.

THORNTON. What a charming house you have. Don't you think so, Pringle?

AUSTIN. Fuck Pringle.

Pause.

THORNTON. I wouldn't say no to a strong Bloody Mary. (*Pause.*) It's just a social visit, I assure you.

AUSTIN. With him in tow?

KATYA goes to the drinks. THORNTON slews round as if examining PRINGLE for the first time.

THORNTON. I do believe the poor chap was on leave. Dragged you up out of a pothole or something, didn't they?

PRINGLE. Das Rheingold, matter of fact.

THORNTON. Yes. Well. I shouldn't tease you, should I? It's just that you people irritate me so. (PRINGLE *is reaching for his briefcase.*) How much did you say Proctor has left?

PRINGLE (*consulting a paper*). About a hundred thousand pounds.

KATYA *brings* THORNTON *a drink, and refills* AUSTIN's *and* VALODYA's *glasses.*

THORNTON. Thank you so much, my dear. (*Sips.*) Yes, there must have been death duties. And all this must have cost a pretty penny. (*Sips.*) Football pools! How *would* you describe this kind of taste, Pringle? (*Sips.*) Red-brick jumped-up Littlewood's.

We hear the Hard Core outside singing 'Happy Birthday to You'. They come stumbling and singing through the glass doors from the garden: SMIDGE, LEN, HENRY (through hall door), GLENDA, GORDON. They cavort round VALODYA, their voices gradually tailing off as they become aware of PRINGLE and THORNTON.

THORNTON. I say. I'm afraid we *are* butting in.

His presence is very authoritative, and the Hard Core wilts shiftily under his steady gaze.

AUSTIN. Another time, then?

Pause. THORNTON *looks at* PRINGLE.

PRINGLE. I don't think so, Mr Thornton.

THORNTON *crosses to* AUSTIN *and stands very close to him. Looks round.*

THORNTON. We *have* let ourselves run downhill a bit, this last eighteen months. (*Drinks.*) Yes. I was shocked when I heard about it, Austin. Simply couldn't believe my ears. (*Pause. Turns to* PRINGLE, *speaking softly.*) Do think of something, Pringle. I'm a scientist, not a doorman —

PRINGLE *is embarrassed but goes to* AUSTIN.

PRINGLE. Would it seem awfully rude if I asked you to chuck these good people out for an hour, Mr Proctor?

Black out.

Scene Six

Fade in. *The sitting room a few minutes later.* THORNTON
stands drumming his fingers on the mantelpiece. PRINGLE
is looking out at the garden. VALODYA *sits relaxed on a couch
with a drink in his hand.* KATYA *is apart from the others.*
PRINGLE *looks at his watch.* THORNTON *notes it.*

THORNTON. You have no tranquillity, Pringle. (*Pause. Crosses
   with his glass to the drinks.*) An excess of phlegm, but you
   are never truly serene. (*Mixing a drink.*) Is it a professional
   thing?

PRINGLE. You did say you were lunching with the Minister.

THORNTON. What he means, Rusakov — is that he has a wife
   and three children in Ruislip. (*He sits down, carefully
   hitching his trousers, and yawns.*) God, what a snob one is!
   (*To* PRINGLE.) Why don't you show him the file your friend
   at the Soviet Embassy gave you last night?

   Pause.

PRINGLE. I don't think so, Sir.

THORNTON. There's an awful rumpus going on in Leningrad
   about you, Vladimir Konstantin —

PRINGLE. Really, Mr Thornton!

THORNTON. Dear me. Was that stuff I read on the way down
   from Cambridge classified?

PRINGLE. As you very well know.

   Pause.

THORNTON. Dear me. (*Pause: as* AUSTIN *enters.*) There you
   are, Austin. (*Drinks.*) Are you marginally sober?

AUSTIN. Need my wife be here for any reason?

THORNTON (*to* PRINGLE). Need she?

PRINGLE. I don't think so.

THORNTON. But I'd be delighted if you'd stay with us though,
   Mrs Proctor. It's not strictly official business. I'd hate to
   think of you sick with worry out there . . . about what's
   going on in here.

AUSTIN (*at* VALODYA). What about him?

THORNTON. Oh, he's neither here *nor* there — is he, Pringle?

PRINGLE. Up to you, Sir.

Pause.

THORNTON. We'll leave it up to him, then. (*Sips.*) He hasn't seen the inside of a physics lab since they took his blackboard and chalk away in nineteen sixty-three. Have you, m'dear feller? (*Goes to the mantelpiece and stands with his hands in his trouser pockets.*) But what a naughty chap you seem to have been in other respects. (*Pause.*) None of our business though, is it, Pringle?

PRINGLE. Hardly.

AUSTIN. What *is* your business, Alan?

THORNTON. Is that a genuine Hockney over there? (*Peering.*) One of his jolly swimming pool efforts in California? I used to spend weekends in Santa Barbara when I was at Los Alamos, you know. What a draughtsman! You should put it down in your little book, Pringle. A hundred thousand quid *and* a Hockney. (*Sips.*) Well. It's really you I'm after, Austin. We want you to come back to work. Yes we do. Isn't that horrid of us?

AUSTIN. Then you might as well bugger off now. I've no intention.

A long pause. THORNTON *crosses to* KATYA.

THORNTON. Shall we raise the tone of the enterprise a little and say *I* want you, Austin. (*To* KATYA.) If he keeps up the drinking you'd have been better off in Israel, wouldn't you? (*Turning to* PRINGLE.) For goodness sake, Pringle, are they Jews or not?

PRINGLE. On the point of matriarchal lineage, she is, Sir — yes.

THORNTON. I mean what the bloody hell have the *Russians* got to say about it?

Pause.

PRINGLE. Rusakov appears to have foxed them with a great deal of false documentation. (*Pause.*) I mean, wearing his knitwear tycoon's hat. (*Pause.*) I mean they haven't, you might say, put the physicist and the black marketeer together. Or they hadn't before he left for Austria, anyway.

VALODYA. Vitamin P.

THORNTON. What's that?

VALODYA. Protektzia.

PRINGLE. Yes. Bribery, in plain English.

VALODYA. I have impression nothing in English is ever plain, Mr Pringle. (*Drinks.*) Like describing yourself yesterday as a 'sort of clerk'.

THORNTON. Shame on you, Pringle —

PRINGLE. What was I supposed to say? I'm a retired Special Branch officer on his uppers? A leg man for the Atomic Energy Authority?

THORNTON. Professor Rusakov. The nearest our pathetic Pringle's been to a bona fide intelligence service is a late-night passion for the novels of John Le Carré. (*Snapping his fingers.*) Let me have the stuff on Proctor, will you?

PRINGLE *roots in his briefcase and hands over a thick file.* THORNTON *waves it in* AUSTIN's *face.*

THORNTON. I must say, it makes depressing and monotonous reading, Austin. (*Pause.*) I never did believe a brilliant man like you quits a distinguished career and starts boozing his head off just because his parents die and he inherits a bit of money. (*He throws the file on a table.*)

AUSTIN. Is that their theory?

He picks up the file.

THORNTON. And it isn't as if you were in weapons research, either.

AUSTIN (*glances in the file — drops it*). I wonder who would . . . bother.

THORNTON. If the CIA can go about trying to poison Fidel Castro's socks, or whatever — what do you think a squalid little outfit like Pringle's can get up to?

VALODYA *gets up with his glass and goes to the drinks.*

VALODYA. Is like old times.

PRINGLE (*sharply*). At least we don't keep the entire population in a state of abject fear in this country. Or practise arbitrary arrest. Or cook up fixed trials in camera. (*Crosses to*

VALODYA.) We don't throw people out of work for their beliefs. Persecute them and their families. Arrange mysterious deaths and beatings on dark nights.

THORNTON. He means of course, hardly ever.

Pause.

VALODYA. I thought you had one and a half million unemployed irrespective of what they believe, Mr Pringle.

THORNTON. Oh foul, Sir! Foul —

VALODYA. Have a drink.

PRINGLE. I damn well will. A large whisky.

VALODYA (*going for the drink*). Yes it was not fair play, Mr Thornton. I think Mr Pringle must have touched some old nerve I thought had withered.

PRINGLE. I didn't mean to go for you. (*Drinks.*) Personally.

VALODYA. Even a Russian who agrees with you can feel cornered. (*Drinks.*) Jumping as we did from the Tsars to Lenin, we missed out, I suppose, a hundred years of civilising bourgeois progress. Yet when American presidents and liberals everywhere assume a high moral tone, the only impressive thing about it to some of my friends in Leningrad is the magnitude of the hypocrisy. And these are men and women who put their safety, their families and their careers at risk every day of their lives. (*Drinks.*) Sometimes we resent that you have this impregnable position, that you are free and we are not. Your society has at least this one incontestable virtue. (*Drinks.*) You will forgive me for grinding my teeth a little. Occasionally this virtue resembles in my opinion — how to put it? - the rectitude of a virgin in her mother's whorehouse. (*Drinks.*) I suspect you intend to blackmail my friend Austin, Mr Thornton. Is that why you come here with your files and so on? I am fascinated. I look to see how it works in a free country.

Pause.

THORNTON. It's frightening what their system does to them mentally. Isn't it? (*Drinks.*) Depressing. How could I possibly blackmail Proctor? He has no public reputation to destroy, and he's done nothing criminal. (*Pause.*) There's almost nothing one *can* get people on, in these amoral times.

PRINGLE. Yes. And laughable though it may seem to exalted folk like Thornton, I really would rather be in Ruislip than wasting my time here. I'm very fond of my wife and children.

THORNTON. Christ, he's boring!

PRINGLE *drains his glass and stands looking at it.*

PRINGLE. I do feel indiscreet all of a sudden.

PRINGLE *crosses and refills his glass.*

PRINGLE. That's breathtaking stuff about you in that Russian dossier, old man. (*Drinks.*) I should say about your Mr Hyde, eh? (*Pats him on the shoulder.*) Stolen knitwear! My goodness me. You got out just in time. (*Drinks.*) They've nicked two of your partners, you know. They're sitting in the Kiev awaiting trial for crimes against the property of the State. (*Grins.*) Trial! Ha! Bang-bang. (*Laughs and slaps* VALODYA's *shoulder.*) Jekyllovitch and Hydeski! (*Holds up the bottle.*) Two of these and I can almost understand Proctor —

THORNTON (*sharply to* AUSTIN). You weren't allowed to gambol through Heathrow Airport yesterday by an oversight, you know —

VALODYA. Gets to sound more and more like situation I left behind. (*Raising his glass.*) But many in Soviet Union would give right arm, so to speak, for English velvet glove.

THORNTON. Look, Austin, you may have married for auld lang syne, or whatever drunken nonsense you and Rusakov were filling each other with in Vienna. But —

KATYA (*standing*). Austin married me because he loves me. This I think you will not find in a dossier.

Pause.

THORNTON. He did?

All eyes turn on AUSTIN. *He stares back mutely.*

THORNTON. That was highly irresponsible.

Pause.

AUSTIN. I think I'm going to hit him, Pringle.

PRINGLE. Be my guest.

THORNTON. Please don't, Austin. I'm deeply touched. (*Drinks.*) Moved, you know? (*To* KATYA.) At the same time,

Mrs Proctor, Vladimir Konstantin — not exactly having married
Austin himself — can be thrown out of this country more or
less at the Home Secretary's discretion. (*To* AUSTIN.) And
yes, of course you could start a public row about it — *but.*
You take my point, Mrs Proctor? (*At* VALODYA.) The shabby
fellow's not quite in the Solzhenitsyn class, now is he? I
can't see the Western liberal conscience being moved by
Rusakov at all. He just isn't inspiring.

Pause.

VALODYA. Why does everybody talk about Solzhenitsyn here?
We know what he has done, what he stands for. That doesn't
mean you have to box every Russian's ears with Solzhenitsyn.
How can you be so arrogant? Alexander Isayevitch is a
religious moralist in a great Russian tradition — but what do
you know about it? You are glib, Mr Thornton. And foolish.
Russia has always thrown up people who yearn for some kind
of revolution of the spirit. That is the meaning of Alexander
Isayevitch. He is not just a flame burning brightly in the
Bolshevik storm. (*Drinks.*) Neither is he a coat-hanger for
the self-righteous ethical tatters of your political system.
(*Pause.*) How corrupt you are!

THORNTON. Now that trips lightly off the tongue of a petty
criminal!

VALODYA. I assure you, Mr Thornton. From Brest Litovsk to
Archangel I did little more than try to correct some of the
failures of our dreadful Soviet distribution system. (*Drinks.*)
Quite a big wheel though, all the same.

THORNTON. There's the further disagreeable fact, Mrs Proctor
— that your father was among those he bribed in the matter of
your exit papers. (*Pause.*) As far as we know this hasn't
come to light over there. But —

KATYA. I know all this.

VALODYA. How does he know it?

THORNTON. How do I know it, Pringle?

PRINGLE. Friend of mine knows one of Proctor's pub cronies.
(*Stares balefully at* AUSTIN.) The Hard Core. (*Pause.*) They
all had quite a session in a local drinking club last night. It's
in the notes I typed up for you this morning. (*Going to refill
his glass.*) I'd ignore the whole stupid charade if I were you,

Proctor. Just tell him to go away. (*Drinks.*)

AUSTIN. Go away. You're even getting on Pringle's nerves.

PRINGLE. There's no sinister plot, Proctor. Nothing official.
There couldn't be. It's all strictly private enterprise.

AUSTIN. Including the files?

PRINGLE. Ah. (*Pause.*) Well. (*Pause.*) They are — to use
Thornton's phrase — bona fide. (*Drinks.*) Copies. (*Drinks.*)
One tries to keep one's hand in, y'know. (*Pointing at*
THORNTON.) Your old boss is on his way out. Needs a little
'coup' of some sort.

AUSTIN. Are you still in your old job or aren't you?

    Pause.

PRINGLE. Well I am in a way, but —

AUSTIN. Professional ambiguity is all?

PRINGLE. Things have got a bit confused in my mind, I'll
admit.

THORNTON. Of course from Pringle's point of view I've
behaved in a most irregular fashion. I did rather spring all this
on him. He's been sullen all the way from Cambridge, and he
doesn't normally drink, I might add.

    PRINGLE *finishes his drink, gathers up the files and puts*
    them in his briefcase.

PRINGLE. I've had enough. I'm off. (*To* THORNTON.) You're
welcome to the car. I'll find a cab. (*Exits.*)

    VALODYA *approaches* THORNTON.

VALODYA. This man worked side by side with Wigner? Under
the same roof? In the same laboratorium?

THORNTON. It's a pity you're out of touch scientifically,
Rusakov. But you were mediocre from the start, weren't you?
(*Pause.*) The Israelis have a most intriguing place at Dimona
in the Negev Desert. You look as if you could do with some
desert air. (*Crossing to* KATYA.) It isn't that your husband's
indispensable, Mrs Proctor. No one is. Or a dazzling genius.
Nothing so romantic. (*Pause.*) There are no doom weapons,
either. No high-energy beams, death rays. That sort of thing's
strictly for paranoid American generals and credulous
journalists. (*Drinks.*) In any case, I don't know that Austin

was ever a man of conscience in the first place. His drinking problem certainly has nothing to do with science. (*Pause.*) It's just that what we were doing together might have turned out awfully prestigious. (*Pause.*) He's left quite a gap in the team. You know how frightfully keen we British are on teams. (*Pause.*) I'm feeling ever so bloody-minded, Austin. (*Drinks.*) Resentful, and vindictive. It must be old age. Never could stand the maverick side of you. (*Pause.*) Let me put it as clearly as I possibly can. (*Pause.*) It's purely personal. I want you and two or three other people — and I'm damn well going to have you. It's simple. Come back to us — or I shall contrive to have him thrown out. (*Going to the door.*) And if you retain a very creditable scepticism about whether this sort of thing really goes on — try me. Even Pringle was never sure whether he could call my possible bluff. (*Pause.*) Are you? (*Exits.*)

VALODYA. What we do now?

Pause.

AUSTIN. We ignore it.

KATYA. You both stood there and heard him out like children!

Pause.

VALODYA. Can we afford to ignore it?

AUSTIN. Oh, come on. He can't get away with something like that.

VALODYA. So why risk to make himself look a fool? (*Pause.*) And why Pringle is helping him?

AUSTIN. Pringle walked out.

VALODYA. He had those documents.

AUSTIN. You're in London, not Leningrad.

VALODYA. I wonder!

AUSTIN. I know Thornton. He's got a paranoid, theatrical streak. (*He fills their glasses.*) Some time ago he had a bee in his bonnet that we were all set for a Nobel Prize. (*Drinks.*) I defected. Alan was furious. He came here and raved and shouted at me about it months ago. I said fuck off. (*Drinks.*) I've been pissed ever since. (*Pause.*) There's half a dozen as good as me, or better. All he has to do is whistle and they'd jump. It's turning into a joint European project. There's Lapotaire in France, Biedermann in Germany, Corbière in Belgium. Thornton's been passed over in all sorts of ways including his knighthood. You know yourself he's done nothing of any consequence since the fifties. He's a burnt-out case when it comes to original research. An administrator. A thwarted old man. He -- (*Pause.*) you mean to say you took all that rubbish seriously?

VALODYA. Pringle was on that plane yesterday.

AUSTIN. If I were you, I'd be a damn sight more worried about your pals in Kiev. (*Drinks.*) If it's true.

VALODYA. Armenians.

AUSTIN. What?

VALODYA. Shmocks.

KATYA. Valodya!

VALODYA. Is true. But I also have Georgian friends. In Tbilisi. (*Drinks.*) Georgian friends will spring Armenian friends. You think criminal genius is by-product of capitalism? Don't believe everything you read in *Pravda*.

AUSTIN. He takes my bloody breath away!

VALODYA. Georgian friends' long fingers reach so far as arsehole of politburo in Moskva.

AUSTIN. I wish I could say the same for mine and the Home Secretary.

Pause.

VALODYA. Yes. Whatever else, I do believe this Thornton could make trouble for me.

AUSTIN. I promise you, it's out of the question. It's a game. A fantasy. It's pathetic, and I'm surprised he bothered to go through the motions.

Pause.

VALODYA. More surprising that Pringle went through the motions. No?

AUSTIN. Who knows what nonsense there is between Thornton and Pringle? Money, sex — I've no idea. I am sure there's no question of an official back-up. (*Pause.*) It'd be ludicrous.

VALODYA. Not in Russia.

AUSTIN. You're not in bloody Russia!

Pause.

VALODYA. So then. We ignore it. (*Pause.*) Austin knows his England. (*Pause.*) I go to pub and gather Hard Core. You remember it is my birthday?

Pause.

AUSTIN. I remember you said you and Katya are leaving. (*Goes to refill his glass.*) And there's an end to the whole idiotic business.

Pause.

VALODYA. We try to make it a good day?

Pause. He goes to hug AUSTIN, *who takes it stiffly.* VALODYA *goes out.*

KATYA. I must go and prepare the food.

Pause.

AUSTIN. I was damned if I was going to say I married you because I loved you.

Pause.

KATYA. I did realise. (*Pause.*) Perhaps I shall get drunk myself this afternoon. (*Shrugs.*) Ach! It is all despicable. (*Pause.*) Coming to your house was an interlude. (*Pause.*) I perhaps imagined a miracle. (*Pause.*) I almost resented it myself, this morning, that Valodya is not one of our respected famous men. (*Pause.*) He could have spit in your Mr Thornton's eye. And then. I was ashamed to think it. (*Pause.*) All the same, he will worry, Austin. (*Pause.*) If it were at home, we would know exactly the meaning of something like this. It doesn't matter if Mr Thornton is playing with us or not. It will prey on Valodya's mind.

AUSTIN. You'll both just have to learn. Won't you?

KATYA (*drily*). To be free?

AUSTIN. To feel free.

Pause.

KATYA. Not just inside our heads!

AUSTIN. Exactly.

Pause.

KATYA. Soon after we arrive in Vienna, I panicked. I asked
myself: despite everything, do I want to be here either?
(*Pause.*) Of course it's amazing. Wonderful at first. So rich,
to our eyes. A feast. (*Pause.*) Then you realise. It has little
relevance to anything you have ever been or thought or
done. (*Pause.*) I bought things. I walked in the city. People
so polite, so correct. Not shabby and ill-tempered. Not fighting
and bickering. (*Pause.*) Just an average day's life can be so
tiring at home. What is more important than money in Russia
is 'blat'. It means something like 'access'. Access to things,
favours, small luxuries, knowing someone who can influence
it for you. (*Pause.*) 'Jumping the queue' do you say? (*Pause.*)
It is a little shocking. In Vienna I realised how much it is
part of our way of life in Russia. We walk a tightrope there,
between the official rules and the ways of trying to make life
just a little more easy. Between official reality and private
reality. (*Pause.*) But the evening of the day before you
arrived, I got back to our hotel and went to my room. I sat
by the window. (*Pause.*) And I suddenly burst into tears.
I thought: I shall be miserable all my life, now. (*Pause.*) I
could have gone back to Leningrad there and then. I was so
homesick. It must sound preposterous. (*Pause.*) I felt this
way last night too. I felt I can never work out my life away
from Russia. (*Pause.*) I didn't come out because you have
some better life in the West. I came out to be with Valodya,
and because I was — tired! (*She begins to sob.*) Tired!

AUSTIN *crosses to the window.*

AUSTIN. I just want to get today over with.

Pause.

KATYA. I thought you did feel something for me in Vienna.

Pause.

AUSTIN. What I'm capable of drunk, and what I'm capable of
sober . . . are two entirely different things. (*Pause.*) The
situation I woke up to yesterday afternoon brought about
what I can only describe as a condition of near-hysterical
disbelief.

Pause.

KATYA. I'm sorry.

Pause.

AUSTIN. Actually. If you drink as much as I do, you're never quite sober at all. (*Pause.*) But that's how I felt.

Pause.

KATYA (*rising*). I'll go and prepare the food, Austin.

She moves towards the door. He is staring out of the window, with his back to her.

AUSTIN. I was twenty years old, at Bikini Atoll. I already had a first in physics. And my ever-so-distinguished professor had — 'blat', shall we say? With the Americans. (*Pause.*) Pringle was there all right. (*Pause.*) He was at the British bomb tests at Monte Bello too. (*Drinks.*) No. Thornton's a fool, or he's going gaga. (*Drinks.*) It's absurd.

KATYA. As strange as the man in our Embassy giving Pringle informations?

Pause.

AUSTIN. When were you born?

KATYA. Today I wish I never had been. (*Exits.*)

Fade out.

Scene Seven.

Fade in. *The sitting room, early evening the same day. The long table is a litter of coffee cups, glasses, piles of dishes, wine bottles, etc. Two large silver candelabra with candles.*

VALODYA, AUSTIN, KATYA *and the Hard Core are disposed about the room — variously somnolent, drunk, well-fed.* PRINGLE *snores very quietly in a chair by the windows, which stand open. The last of the sun makes a golden light in the room. It is peaceful, mellow, and there is very faint nostalgic music.* SMIDGE *is twirling a flower,* ANNIE *looking at an impressive black eye in her compact mirror.* GLENDA *drunkenly lowers herself to the arm of* VALODYA's *chair.*

GLENDA. I've changed my mind. I think he's beautiful. (*Drinks.*) I think being Russian is beautiful in itself. It's enough. It's ideal. (*Drinks.*) It's poetic.

Pause.

LEN. I've always fancied Henry, myself.

GORDON (*A long, satisfied belch.*)

SMIDGE (*to* ANNIE). Is it painful, dear?

ANNIE. You should see what I did to my old man. Dislocated his jaw, I shouldn't wonder.

SMIDGE. Accusing you of adultery like that!

LEN. I hear the same story day in day out. (*Drinks.*) If we've got a permissive society, why does half of London seem to be accusing the other half of adultery? Ask any private eye. They'll all tell you the same story. (*Drinks.*) When they're in work, that is.

Pause.

SMIDGE. It's been a lovely party.

GORDON. What d'you mean, been? It's only just starting.

LEN. There's a wonderful atmosphere in your house tonight, Austin. (*Pause.*) Lived in. (*Pause.*) Always fancied Henry, I have. I've been thinking it over, and I've decided I ought to come out, you know.

GORDON. Cor Christ listen to him! They've been on to you at the Fox since before gay liberation was invented, Len. (*Pulls at his cigar.*) It's always been a tolerant pub.

LEN (*pointing his cigar at* PRINGLE). And this one's a funny bugger as well, if you ask me.

GORDON. Not your bloody way he isn't.

LEN. I've never had a lover.

GORDON (*rising, going to the window*). I think it's time our Henry came out as well. Why don't you take him upstairs and bang him, Henry?

HENRY. If I wasn't too drunk to get up, I'd kill you.

SMIDGE. It has been a lovely party though.

GORDON. Just you sit there quietly an' pull your flower, will you?

GLENDA (*at* VALODYA). I think I'll marry him.

GORDON *is looking down at* PRINGLE. *He removes a glass from his rigid fingers.*

GORDON. You can tell he's not Hard Core.

LEN. Definitely.

GORDON. I mean he didn't survive the pub session, did he? (*Pause.*) I had to cut his fucking shashlik for him, did you notice? (*Pause.*) By God it was a tip top dinner, Katya. I don't suppose they'll eat like that very often in Russia. (*Pause.*) Fucking Krushchev —

SMIDGE. A little bit less of the F-U-C-K-ing if you don't mind, Gordon.

GLENDA. Will you marry me, Valodya?

VALODYA. It means British passport?

GORDON. You know, I look out there. I watch the sun setting. And I think of all the Hard Cores all over England. (*Drinks.*) Decent men and women enjoying a well-earned drink. (*Pause.*) When you come to think about it, we're the last bulwark between this government and total bloody slavery. (*Drinks.*) I don't care what they say.

ANNIE (*in full voice*). Land of hope and glory, Mother of the free —

Pause.

SMIDGE. A lovely, stirring song, don't you think?

GORDON. It'll be gone in a minute.

LEN. What will?

GORDON. The sun, you stupid bastard.

VALODYA. Is only great ball of burning hydrogen, Gordon —

GORDON. That may well be your limited point of view. Far as I'm concerned it was put there — I mean over there on the bloody horizon — to signal the hour for some serious drinking. Chota peg time, Henry eh? You peevish little eunuch.

HENRY. If I wasn't paralysed all down one side, I'd kill him.

KATYA *begins to light the candles.*

SMIDGE. We never have candles.

GORDON. We wouldn't dare have 'em in the house, would we?

SMIDGE. He's so vulgar.

PRINGLE slowly returns to consciousness, sits forward and begins to polish his glasses with a handkerchief.

PRINGLE. Well. What about it then, Rusakov? (*Pause.*) Austin?

GORDON. Chota peg time in Leningrad hours ago. (*Pause.*) Chota: Hindi, meaning small or young. Peg: a tot of whisky — no? (*Pause.*) Evening star time. There it is. Makes me feel quite lyrical. (*Pause.*) We gave a bit of thought to your problem, Austin. In the pub. (*Pointing at* PRINGLE.) He was in there drinking the place dry long before you arrived. 'This can't possibly be Ruislip,' he kept saying. (*Pause.*) Another one that doesn't drink.

AUSTIN. I have a problem?

GORDON. The commissar there was telling Henry.

Pause.

VALODYA. Interesting fellow, Henry. (*Pause.*) He is only one of you knew I had bribed Katya's father — who certainly does nothing out of family feeling. (*Pause.*) Did I not tell you about it, Henry? (*Pause.*) And today Mr Pringle knows. Mr Thornton knows. (*Pause.*) Who doesn't know, I wonder?

Pause.

GORDON (*peering out*). All that muck up there in the heavens. Twinkling. Spinning. Rotating. (*Drinks.*) Orbits. Elliptics. (*Drinks.*) Ah, merciless indifferent Nature!

GORDON fills his glass and goes to the piano. Strikes a few chords. Plays and sings an old Tom Lehrer song: 'I have a friend in Omsk, who has a friend in Tomsk; whose friend in Ashmolinsk, has other friend in Minsk'. He stops with a flourish. Drinks. Looks round at them, grinning.

GORDON. An East German dog's going on at a West German dog about how marvellous it is in East Germany. Health, education, housing — the lot. After a bit the West German dog gets uptight and says: If it's so bloody marvellous over there, what you doing here in West Berlin? (*Drinks.*) Ah, says the East German dog, they let you bark over here —

He starts playing and singing the Eton boating song. Stops. Drinks.

GORDON. Two workers: one Russian, the other English.
'Capitalism', says the Russian worker, 'is the exploitation of
man by man'. 'Ho yes', says the English worker, 'and what's
communisr.; then?' (*Drinks*.) 'Communism', says the Russky,
'is exactly the opposite'. (*Pause*.) For God's sake cheer up,
you lot.

Pause.

AUSTIN. Did you know it was Henry, Pringle?

PRINGLE. No.

HENRY *is ashen, sober.*

HENRY. I can explain, Austin.

AUSTIN. Can you now?

Pause.

HENRY. Old friend of mine. Agreed to ring him now and then.
(*Pours a drink*.) Friend from way back, you know. (*Drinks*.)
Army days. (*Drinks*.) Decent man. I'm no informer, you
know. He asked about you. About your drinking. (*Drinks*.)
Great loss to science and all the rest of it. Everybody very
worried about you. (*Drinks*.) Would I keep an eye. (*Pause*.)
Yes, I would, I said. Fond of old Austin. Boozing pals.
(*Pause*.) Bit gone to seed myself, I said. Got to look after
each other, haven't we? (*Pause*.) That's right, he said. Take
care of him. (*Pause*.) Ring me now and then. (*Pause*.) It's
nothing official. Can't do any harm though, keeping an
eye. (*Pause*.) Yes, on you, Austin. On you. (*Pause*.) Your
health, he meant. I mean, your condition – you know?
(*Pause*.) How you are, so to speak –

Pause.

AUSTIN. You phoned him last night?

Pause.

HENRY. In the small hours. Pissed. (*Pause*.) Who wasn't?
(*Pause*.) I didn't want to ring *him*, d'you see. (*Pause*.) I was
sitting by my window with a glass of scotch. I'm sorry,
Austin, I – oh my God. I was sitting up there, my head
reeling. My eyes full of tears, suddenly. (*Pause*.) I just wanted
to ring somebody and talk. And tell them. (*Pause*.) I want to
blow my fucking brains out, I wanted to say. (*Pause*.) You
can imagine how many phone numbers there are in *my* little

book. (*Drinks.*) There you are, so I rang this chap. (*Pause.*) And instead of blabbing about suicide, I raved on about the situation here. (*Pause.*) He was very kind, actually —

Pause.

AUSTIN. Why on earth do you want to blow your brains out, Henry? They've never done anything to you. (*Drinks.*) Or for you, either.

Pause.

HENRY. You're not angry?

AUSTIN. Oh well, you've abused my hospitality and my good nature it's true. (*Drinks.*) But I'm not one to impose conventions on those around me. (*Looking around.*) Otherwise I'd hardly tolerate you all, would I? (*Pause.*) Where would we all be if we had the slightest genuine feeling for each other? (*Drinks.*) Certainly not in the Hard Core. (*Drinks.*) Certainly not sitting here drinking hail and farewell to my Russian friend. Who with his charming relative is so soon to quit our boozy circle. So soon to try it on elsewhere. (*Pause.*) The Negev Desert has been suggested.

Pause.

SMIDGE. It's a beastly way to talk, Austin. Gordon and I are very fond of you. Aren't we, Gordon?

GLENDA (*to* VALODYA). Are you going because of that business with (*at* PRINGLE) him and that other man?

PRINGLE *gets up and stands blinking, cleaning his glasses.*

PRINGLE. I don't know what you all know, or think you know.

AUSTIN. Eustace William Harold Pringle will now assert his credibility.

Pause.

VALODYA. I would say we leave because there is failure of psychological navigation system. (*Pause.*) Katya and I do not understand. We are not understood. (*Pause.*) If this with Mr Pringle, Mr Thornton and my dear friend Austin is some complex British kind of charade, I can only say my fear is a high price to pay for enjoying your sense of humour. (*Pause.*) Perhaps the difference is that we have known what we fear. For you it is an act of imagination. (*Pause.*) Perhaps never quite real.

GORDON (*playing and singing*). There's an old mill by the stream, Nelly Dean — *etc.*

ANNIE *totters to the piano with a bottle, fills their glasses and joins* GORDON *in full voice.*

ANNIE and GORDON.
And the waters as they flow
Seem to whisper soft and low —
You're my heart's delight,
I love you, Nelly Dean.

GLENDA (*screaming*). Stop it!

Pause.

PRINGLE. I stand here. I look around at all of you. (*Pause.*) I think to myself: there's two worlds, Pringle. (*Gets himself a drink.*) Yours is the one on top, so to speak. Up there in the sunshine, where people try to get on with life. (*Pause.*) Then there's the one underneath, populated with shabby anonymous citizens like me — and their masters — whose drab justification is that if we didn't do your dirty work, you wouldn't be able to lead the life you do. (*Drinks.*) Beavering away, you might say . . . that the fear Rusakov so poignantly recalls, will never be a condition of your existence. (*Drinks. Looks round.*) I'm not the only one to ask myself from time to time if you're all worth it — worth, I mean, the abdication of every value, scruple and moral conviction the small long-ago Pringle had drummed into him at school, church and mother's knee. (*Pause.*) Sad fact is though, you seem to me a fairly representative sample. You and yours are what it's all about. (*Drinks.*) You're the human vomit coughed up by the democracy I've so often dirtied my hands for. (*Crossing to* AUSTIN.) I owed Alan Thornton a favour, Austin. (*Pause.*) When you were still scraping your little knees on the rugger field, Thornton's brother once led the Gestapo away from me. And was never seen again. (*Crosses to* HENRY.) As for this sodden little rat — his Whitehall friend, on whom he so depends by telephone at three, four and five in the morning. His friend has been doing him favours for decades. (*Bending over* HENRY.) Lovers, weren't you? (*Gesturing to them all.*) And Captain Henry Craxton dishonoured the man without batting an eyelid, to save his own commission. (*Drinks.*) Oh yes, I did know it was Henry, Austin. It's unimportant. I'm glad you seem to think

so too. You're the offended party. Only, I couldn't pass up
the chance to offend you myself. You're one of those people
who acquire a myth, over the years — in the total absence, so
far as I can make out, of either character or personality.
(*Drinks.*) Proctor the genius. Proctor the white hope of
controlled fusion. The man without a private life. The man
so scarred by nihilism and despair (thus goes your curriculum
vitae), that his lethal intelligence finds peace only in the
mathematics of those vast, subatomic spaces. (*Drinks.*) Shit,
Proctor. I've been in the business of private lives for decades
till I took to opera, my garden, and the study of edible fungi.
(*Drinks.*) Shit again, Proctor. All you are is a fifty-year-old
grammar school boy with a huge, maniacal gift in one
microscopic corner of science. (*He throws down his glass and
grabs* AUSTIN, *hauling him to his feet.*) I didn't like your
performance in Vienna one little bit!

He pushes AUSTIN *back into his chair, seizes a bottle and
drinks from the neck.* GORDON *begins to play and sing 'As
Time Goes By'.* ANNIE *joins in.* SMIDGE *joins in.* GLENDA
joins in. Slowly, VALODYA *rises. He stands in the centre of
the room, and by sheer force of presence causes them to
falter. He waits until he has complete silence.*

VALODYA. What a commendable fellow Mr Pringle is! (*Pause.*)
At eleventh hour, at brink of abyss — he flaunts a nostalgia
for something human! (*Drinks.*) I have to admit, Soviet Union
does not turn out KGB men of such calibre. (*Pause.*)
Katyushka, shall we begin to pack at once? (*Pause.*) I am a
little sick.

KATYA *crosses to* AUSTIN *and looks down at him. He
stares back at her glassily. He puts his hands out towards
her. She sits facing him, just out of reach.* PRINGLE *crosses
to* VALODYA.

PRINGLE. I genuinely am retired, old man. (*Pats his shoulder.*)
You really shouldn't make odious comparisons, you know.
(*Pause.*) Let's have a bit of a practical joke with young
Proctor, Thornton said. (*Drinks.*) Jolt him out of his apathy.
Put the wind up him. (*Pause.*) Ah, I said. Those Russians
won't find it very funny, dear old prick. (*Drinks.*) You won't
have them in fits, I said. (*Drinks.*) Fuck them, he said. They're
nobody.

He stands swaying, a hand on VALODYA's *shoulder.*

PRINGLE. Come off it, Rusakov. I did walk out when the joke turned sour. (*Pause.*) Oh really, dear old chap, I've given Proctor his what for, haven't I?

Pause.

VALODYA. In my opinion, Mr Thornton was serious. (*Pause.*) In my opinion, he hoped the marriage between Austin and Katya was not an affair of convenience. (*Pause.*) In my experience, such as you never retire, Mr Pringle. (*Pause.*) My conviction is that you are an accomplished liar, a subtle clown, but nobody's fool.

Pause.

PRINGLE. I wonder what Mrs Proctor thinks? (*Drinks.*) If Proctor's the offended party — I'd say she's the injured party.

Pause.

KATYA. What I think? (*Pause.*) I think I shall go back to my own country.

GLENDA. Don't put yourself out on my account, darling!

AUSTIN *has been struggling to get up. He drains his glass and faces* KATYA.

AUSTIN. You won't, you know —

Pause.

KATYA. It's too late, Austin.

He slumps back into his chair, fumbling for a bottle. Slowly, KATYA *walks past them hesitating in front of each one, then moving on. As she passes* GLENDA:

GLENDA (*raising her glass*). Get thee to a Gulag!

As KATYA *stares at her,* GLENDA's *garish smile seems trapped on her face.*

PRINGLE. Ah, it's hopeless you know —

Pause.

KATYA. I am not hopeless.

PRINGLE. I've no idea what I meant, actually.

He drifts away to find another drink.

GLENDA. They're quite soft on people who choose to go back. (*Drinks.*) So I've heard.

KATYA. It doesn't matter, one way or the other.

GLENDA. What does, darling?

SMIDGE. I thought they made a lovely couple.

GORDON. Silly fart!

SMIDGE. Must be lovely, if one of you's sober now and then. (*She starts crying — a look from* GORDON *stops her.*) Touching, really —

KATYA. A Spanish communist said long ago: better to die on your feet than live on your knees. (*Pause.*) I think I would rather fight on my knees, in Russia — than one day to die in your kind of freedom. (*Pause.*) Heartbroken.

She exits. GORDON *strikes a chord or two and calls out plaintively.*

GORDON. Can we get on with the party now?

SMIDGE. I feel ever so sorry for her.

GORDON. It's their educational system. (*Drinks.*) It's like the Jesuits say. (*Drinks.*) They get 'em young and they've got 'em for life. (*Pause.*) Brainwashed.

Pause.

GLENDA. Well, little old Cousin Vladimir. What about you then?

VLADIMIR *crosses to* AUSTIN — *who sprawls in his chair, half comatose.*

VALODYA. Austin —

AUSTIN. Welcome to my house —

He slides a little further down in his chair. GLENDA *goes to stand behind his chair and leans over him, ruffling his hair.*

GLENDA. He's a defector himself, in his way. Aren't you, sweetie? (*She stares wryly at* VALODYA.) But Glenda still wants him. (*She folds her arms round him.*) Glenda's afraid of the big, wide, bleak world outside Austin's house.

GLENDA *moves round and drapes herself across* AUSTIN's *lap, with a bottle and a glass.*

VALODYA. I a defector? (*Pause.*) In other circumstances Lenin called it voting with your feet.

GLENDA. Well. Little Katya isn't exactly voting with her head — is she?

VALODYA looks round. GORDON is slumped at the piano. ANNIE is propped against it, her head down over her arms and still clutching a glass. LEN is asleep. PRINGLE is nodding off. HENRY sits twisting a napkin, oblivious to everything. SMIDGE is snoring gently. AUSTIN's head is thrown back on his chair — GLENDA is holding a glass to his lips. She grasps him by the hair at the back of his head and tilts it forwards like a ventriloquist's dummy.

GLENDA. Say goodbye to your nice friend from Leningrad —

AUSTIN. Goodbye —

She lets go. His head falls back. She presses her mouth to his. GORDON releases a long, slow, reverberating belch. GLENDA turns to VALODYA.

GLENDA. Shouldn't you be packing?

Pause.

HENRY. Whenever my father's wits and imagination failed him, he used to run away. Another country. Assumed name. (*Pause.*) He was a well-travelled man. (*To* VALODYA.) Time for me to move on. (*Crosses to stand looking down at* AUSTIN.) One last binge, eh? (*He touches* AUSTIN's *cheek* — GLENDA *pushes his hand away.*) You know, Valodya. Even as late in the imperial day as my army youth, we had a keen sense of disgrace. (*Moves behind* AUSTIN's *chair, touches his head.*) I've seen men walk away from life as he did. (*Drinks.*) It's a disgrace. A dishonour. (*Pause.*) To turn one's back. (*Pause.*) I demeaned myself to the role of a servant, for Austin. (*Pause.*) To care for him. (*Pause.*) All very platonic. (*Pause.*) I had a thing for one or two brother officers. But I never touched a man sexually. (*Looking from* AUSTIN *to* VALODYA.) I've dishonoured the two of you. And myself as well —

He goes to the window, filling his glass on the way, and stands looking out. AUSTIN comes to, pushing at GLENDA. She slides off him and away to a chair to sulk drunkenly.

AUSTIN. Get off me! (*Pause.*) I'd get up, Valodya — if I could. (*He struggles to his feet.*) A tune, Gordon! What about a reel? A tango?

He finds a drink and shudders as he downs it.

AUSTIN. I'm full of hope, really. But it's a spiritual achievement rather than a plan of campaign. (*Drinks.*) It's my wife. Her decision. It raises me up, d'you see? To new heights of incredulity. (*Drinks.*) I find such monumental foolishness inspiring. (*He lurches to* VALODYA *and thumps him on the shoulder.*) She does precisely what Thornton says you don't, Valodya. She inspires —

He pats VALODYA *patronisingly on the shoulder once or twice, and ambles about looking for a bottle.*

AUSTIN. They'll put the red carpet down for her in Leningrad. You'll see. (*Pouring.*) I wonder if she'll catch on? (*Drinks.*) I doubt it. (*Drinks.*) What are you going to do? Shoot yourself? Hang yourself in the garden? (*Drinks.*) Do Russians still snuff it at the drop of a hat — as appears to be mandatory in the literature? (*Pause.*) You know, if Thornton did have you thrown out — just, shall we say, as a valedictory gesture of malice towards me — I wouldn't lift a finger. (*Drinks.*) The letter columns of *The Times* and *The Guardian* would be safe from old Proctor, I can tell you. (*Pause.*) Go on — do yourself in! I'll write your epitaph: Here lies one whose name was writ in knitwear.

Pause.

VALODYA. I shall go with Katya.

AUSTIN. Oh, come come! Two or three days in this unique environment's hardly the critical basis for a rejection of the entire Western world, is it? (*Drinks.*) Goodness me!

VALODYA *crosses to him, standing close.* AUSTIN *sways and smiles.*

VALODYA. I go with her because she is right.

AUSTIN. Dear old sport — (*He gestures at the others.*) we aren't a valid statistical sample, you know. By no stretch of the imagination.

Pause.

VALODYA. Do you realise how courageous she is?

AUSTIN. Oh, quite. (*Drinks.*) I'm deeply moved.

Pause.

VALODYA. I am.

Pause.

AUSTIN. I see. You got into England on my back. I suppose you visualise rehabilitation in Russia on hers. (*Drinks.*) Prodigal children!

Pause.

VALODYA. Katya is right.

AUSTIN. What a fickle chap you are!

VALODYA. In the end it is quite simple. (*Pause.*) This I did conclude for myself in two or three days — as you put it. (*Pause.*) The moral struggle in the Soviet Union is one thing for us and another thing for you. (*Pause.*) Cousin Vladimir is not inspiring? How do you think you seem to Katya? For one thing, an educated Russian her age probably sees you as an appalling case of weakness — there being no such thing in our country as a young mind made subtle by the insights of Freud. We had our so-called superfluous man in the nineteenth century — and quite enough of him thank you very much, she might say. (*He smiles thinly.*) Despair we know. Austerity, persecution, violence and murder — these we grew up with. (*Pause.*) Katya was ten when Stalin died. I have no doubt she shed tears. (*Pause.*) Now she knows the truth. And she knows the mystification and brutishness have never ceased. Only become less extreme, or shall we say more refined in method. (*Pause.*) She can say to herself: we have all been incorporated into the Soviet lie. How to fight our way out of it? (*Pause.*) I believe she only stayed in Vienna for my sake. And what did you and I do with her? (*Pause.*) Into what lie are you and I incorporated, in our different ways? (*Pause.*) I only begin to truly love Katya since I see her watching you, Austin. I feel like anxious, loving, humble father towards her. (*Pause.*) I am born again, as the religious could say. It is a matter for pain and remorse in my eyes that you are not in fact moved by her at all. (*Pause.*) At least I can say to Leningrad authorities — it is my fault. She would not have done this without me. (*Pause.*) I don't condemn you. I am amazed and frightened by you. (*Pause.*) Forgive me, Austin, but your anguish suddenly seems trivial to me. (*He goes to the door slowly.*) Curious. (*Turns.*) I think I am happy, now. (*Pause.*) It is possible, one day our own sense of freedom will break out of Russian skulls and into the light. (*Pause.*) By our own efforts. (*Pause.*) I think we should try to avoid tainting ourselves with your approval. (*Pause.*) From the little I see in Europe, your freedom is something you do not know what to do with. (*Pause.*) I hope I shall live to be a very old man, to watch my Katya's heart grow — as yours has surely shrivelled.

He goes out. GORDON *strikes a few loud chords. One by one they all come to life.*

GORDON. Is this a party or isn't it?

AUSTIN *stands transfixed, looking at the door.* ANNIE *takes him by the arm and leads him to the piano. They all fill their glasses and gather round.* GORDON *launches with great verve into: 'Hello, Hello — Who's Your Lady Friend?' etc.*

Curtain.

SHOOTING
THE CHANDELIER

Shooting the Chandelier was first presented by BBC Television on BBC-2 on 26 October 1977. The cast was as follows:

RUSSIAN SOLDIER	Dave Atkins
SIMON (Semyon Vasilievich Rusakov)	Denholm Elliott
BLANKA (Blanka Soltesz)	Felicity Dean
MILENA	Doris Hare
NIKOLAI (Colonel Shchetkin)	Edward Fox
BRODOVICH	Alun Armstrong
PEASANT	Ernest Jenkins

Produced by Margaret Matheson
Directed by Jane Howell
Designed by Richard Henry

1. Exterior. Sky. Night. *The stunning flash and sound of heavy guns firing. Salvo after salvo, with split seconds of absolute silence. On black screen in the moments of silence:*

2. Exterior. Sky. Morning. *A clear, brilliant azure sky. A lark hangs in the blue air, singing.*

3. Exterior. Country Road. Morning. *A winding road in flat country. A RUSSIAN SOLDIER wobbles precariously on a bicycle. He is helmeted but in shirt sleeves. On each bare forearm, from wrist to elbow, are strapped several watches. There is the sound of bells pealing all over the countryside. The SOLDIER stops the bicycle and sits there listening. He pulls a bottle of vodka from a pack on his back and drinks. Finishes the bottle.*
  We follow him as he pushes off again, wobbling from side to side down the dusty road, the bicycle creaking noisily.

4. Exterior. Country Road. Ditch. Morning. *A middle-aged man — SIMON RUSAKOV — in the dirty and battle-stained uniform of a Junior Field Officer lies drunk. In one hand he clutches a battered map case, pressed to his chest. In the other, an empty bottle. He is snoring loudly.*

5. Exterior. Country House. Morning. *A large, impressive, nineteenth-century house — almost a schloss, and built in the style of one. It has an air of neglect, broken windows — out of one of which a thin spume of smoke drifts up into the spring sky. There are wide steps down from heavy double doors, and a drive rutted and scored with the careless manoeuvrings of army vehicles. The drive curves in a horseshoe shape from the front of the house, enclosing lawns, trees, terraces.*
  Near the front of the house — the sandbagged entrance to a bunker. From this black opening emerge two women: a girl of eighteen — BLANKA — and a woman in her sixties — MILENA. Both are in rough clothes, dishevelled, bewildered.
  BLANKA walks slowly, timidly, across the lawn and stands looking at the deserted house. She looks up at the sky: the lark

is there, singing. And far away, the sound of the bells.
   BLANKA *turns to* MILENA, *half laughing, half crying.*

BLANKA. They've gone, Milena! The Germans have gone —

   MILENA *is brushing at her long black dress and looks up at
   the girl sourly.*

MILENA. I'm hungry. Aren't you?

BLANKA (*kissing her*). The Germans have *gone!*

MILENA (*looking at the house*). It looks like it. Now all we
   have to do is wait for the Russians.

BLANKA. But it means the war is over. (*Pause.*) Listen —

   Pause.

MILENA. What?

BLANKA. There's a lark singing. High up there. (*Pause.*) It's
   wonderful. It's amazing.

MILENA. Oh yes? Well I wonder if the Red heroes have
   liberated Brno? Because that's where I'm going. To my
   sister's. And that's where I'm taking you, Blanka.

   BLANKA *turns on her angrily.*

BLANKA. Oh no you aren't! We're staying here. We're going
   to live here. (*Pause.*) This was my parents' house. Now it's
   mine, surely?

   Pause.

MILENA. Don't you understand anything at all?

BLANKA (*laughing*). I understand everything. *Everything* —

   *And she runs up the lawn, across the drive, up the steps and
   through the half-open front doors.*
      MILENA *stands looking round — the gracious if
   dilapidated gardens, the fields and woods beyond. We hear the
   bells pealing loudly, and* MILENA *makes her way reluctantly
   after* BLANKA.

6. Exterior. Country Road. Ditch. Morning. SIMON RUSAKOV
*has pulled himself halfway out of the ditch, and there his
hangover has hit him with full force. The upper half of his body
is sprawled over the rough grass verge of the road. His legs dangle*

in the ditch. He is blinking at the strong light and trying to moisten his cracked lips.

7. Exterior. Country Road. Morning. *A Russian jeep is heading in RUSAKOV's direction. In it: a fresh and smart looking Russian colonel, wearing the olive green cap of the NKVD, and a DRIVER. The officer is NIKOLAI SHCHETKIN: fair, bony, about thirty years old. From Shchetkin's point of view:*

8. Exterior. Country Road. Ditch. Morning. RUSAKOV, *laboriously heaving himself out of the ditch and on to the road. The jeep pulls up and NIKOLAI leans out. He and SIMON stare at each other.*

NIKOLAI. Well well well!

SIMON. Oh my God!

He manages to get to his knees. NIKOLAI gets out of the jeep and stands over him.

NIKOLAI. Professor Rusakov! My dear old professor! (*Pause: bends down.*) Are we ill, Semyon Vasilievich?

SIMON. Acutely.

NIKOLAI helps him up, and makes a show of dusting at SIMON's uniform.

NIKOLAI. And — are we, how shall I put it? Lost?

SIMON. Irretrievably.

NIKOLAI stands smiling at him, then slowly looks round the countryside.

NIKOLAI. But isn't it a beautiful morning, though?

SIMON. I can't see it all that well.

He is still somehow clutching the map case. NIKOLAI gently takes it from him, opens it and holds it upside down. It is empty.

SIMON (*hoarsely*). Nikolai —

NIKOLAI. You seem to have lost your maps, too.

NIKOLAI hands back the map case and climbs into the jeep. SIMON stands miserably in the road: dusty, crumpled, his greying hair standing up in sweaty spikes, his face puffy, his intelligent eyes hopeless.

NIKOLAI. I think we shall have to get you to a doctor.

SIMON. Oh, I don't think that's . . . well really please don't trouble. (*Pause.*) I wouldn't bother, you know.

NIKOLAI. But it grieves me to see you in this condition. It really grieves me. (*Pause.*) Rusakov ill in his ditch while history, so to speak, flows round him. (*Pause.*) Do you know what day — what the date is, Semyon Vasilievich?

Pause.

SIMON. Er — April 24th?

NIKOLAI. Correct. And yesterday, the 53rd Army took Pratzen.

Pause.

SIMON (*glumly*). How splendid!

NIKOLAI. I would have thought you, as a professor of history —

SIMON. I know, I know. Pratzen was the site of the Battle of Austerlitz.

NIKOLAI. An inspiring thought?

SIMON. Even Stalin could hardly take any credit for Austerlitz.

There is a long grim silence. SIMON *scuffles at the road with one filthy, chewed-looking boot.*

NIKOLAI. You haven't changed much, have you?

SIMON. Absolutely not at all. (*Sudden, cheerful smile.*) Isn't it regrettable?

Pause.

NIKOLAI. Might one ask? Mere curiosity, nothing more. Which army you are with? (*Pause.*) You do know which army you are with?

SIMON. 6th Infantry Division. Major-General Obushenko commanding.

NIKOLAI. Any idea where they are?

SIMON *peers around the quiet, innocent countryside as if expecting to find the 6th Infantry there somewhere. He waves vaguely North-West.*

SIMON. Somewhere over there, I should imagine.

NIKOLAI. Semyon Vasilievich —

SIMON. Do call me 'Simon'. As you used to. (*Pause.*) As all you bright young men and women used to.

NIKOLAI *lights a cigarette and regards* SIMON *sternly.*

NIKOLAI. I'll bet you wish you could just climb back into that ditch and stay there until it's all over!

SIMON. How perceptive you are, Nikolai. (*Pause.*) Always were, as I remember.

NIKOLAI. Well, *Simon.* The 4th Guards Cavalry Corps, the 7th Mechanised Corps, the 6th Guards Tank Army — and *your 6th Infantry Division,* are preparing at this moment for the liberation of Brno.

Pause.

SIMON. Oh dear!

Pause.

NIKOLAI. Prague will fall to us within two weeks, I should say.

Pause.

SIMON. This map case. It isn't mine. I picked it up somewhere.

NIKOLAI. Oh yes?

SIMON. Yes indeed. And as for me —

NIKOLAI. As for you?

SIMON. Well, I'm just a cook really. Hardly anything more than a sort of glorified cook. (*Pause.*) Not inside my head, of course. In there I'm still very historical. And philosophical. And all the rest of it. But my actual body — dear young Nikolai, dear friend — my actual body . . . well it *cooks.* (*Pause.*) Though I have worked my way up from the kitchens to the paperwork.

The DRIVER — *hitherto immobile* — *turns and regards* SIMON *with a look of total disbelief.*
    NIKOLAI *is smiling his tight smile.* NIKOLAI *taps the side of the jeep.*

NIKOLAI. Get in.

Pause.

SIMON. How extraordinary to run into one of one's old students like this! Bang in the middle of a war.

NIKOLAI. Get in, Semyon Vasilievich.

Pause.

SIMON (*hesitantly*). I'm extremely frightened, you know.

NIKOLAI. Of what, Comrade?

Pause.

SIMON. Of you, Nikolai.

NIKOLAI. Oh, come come! What's one poor, sick, lost cook — among all these troublesome Czechs?

SIMON. *Are* they troublesome?

NIKOLAI. Look. Either get in and I'll see what I can do for you. Or go your own way and leave me compelled to report you. (*He looks at his watch.*) We've wasted enough time.

SIMON. I certainly couldn't go my own way, Nikolai. I've never known what it was. (*Pause.*) Getting lost you know — it's the only weak little flair I have in life.

Pause.

NIKOLAI. So we all noticed at the University!

SIMON *grins sheepishly, climbs into the jeep, and they drive off.*

9. Interior. Country house. Ballroom. Afternoon. *A long, finely proportioned room, with tall windows overlooking a terrace. It is grimy and cobwebby — the windows dirty and cracked, some of them hanging open — but the gilt and blue and white of eighteenth-century pastiche still show.*

BLANKA *enters with an old-fashioned winding gramophone in her arms and some records. She sets it on the floor, winds it, and puts on one of the records: a nostalgic, pre-war waltz. She begins to dance, with a certain pathetic dignity — and obvious pleasure.*

10. Interior. Country house. Kitchen. Afternoon. *A large kitchen, solidly furnished, which must have been very handsome pre-war. Now it is filthy: pots and pans everywhere, remnants of food peelings, tins, greasy dishes, doors hanging off cupboards. A large German calendar on one wall showing the month of April, 1945: a sort of Wagnerian idealised blonde woman with* *one breast bared in a long theatrical dress. There is kitchen garbage all over the tiled floor, and in one corner a small white mongrel dog is rooting in an overturned pail full of slops.*

MILENA *enters and confronts the mess with a look of impassive hostility. She goes to the dog and kicks it. Squealing, it runs out through the open door which gives onto a large kitchen garden.*

MILENA *straightens an overturned chair by the long wooden table, and sits looking round the kitchen.*

11. Exterior. Country house. Afternoon. *The jeep with* SIMON, NIKOLAI *and the* DRIVER *comes up the drive and stops in front of the steps.* SIMON *is fast asleep, his mouth hanging open.*

NIKOLAI *sits looking up at the house for a moment. Then he shakes* SIMON *by the arm.* SIMON *groans.*

NIKOLAI. Give him some vodka.

The DRIVER *takes a small flat canteen and holds it under* SIMON's *nose. He wakes up, takes the canteen and swallows hard.*

SIMON. Where are we?

NIKOLAI *gets out of the jeep and stands looking at the house, the grounds. The* DRIVER *starts unloading various items:* NIKOLAI's *personal baggage, three flat padlocked tin boxes, a crate of wine, half a smoked pig wrapped in muslin, a crate of assorted vegetables, two submachine guns.*

NIKOLAI. This is how they used to live, Semyon Vasilievich.

SIMON. Who? The rotten old bourgeoisie?

NIKOLAI *turns and looks down at him, his face expressionless.*

NIKOLAI. You know. One can't help wondering how you survived the nineteen thirties. (*Pause.*) Innocent. Honest. Scholarly. (*Pause.*) Absolutely scrap material, from a revolutionary point of view. (*Pause.*) Intellectual scum.

SIMON. There had to be *some* survivors. Even from a merely statistical point of view. (*Pause.*) One kept one's head down you know, Nikolai —

NIKOLAI. So did thousands of others. But it didn't help them in the end. (*Pause.*) I suppose you kept your head so far down

that there were plenty of influential boots within reach of
your tongue!

SIMON. What was the point of being heroic? Would it have been
heroic? (*Pause.*) I started shivering with fright in nineteen
twenty-nine, and I haven't stopped yet. (*He holds up his
hand.*) Look —

NIKOLAI *stares distastefully at the trembling hand. He turns
away, gazing towards the house once more. The* DRIVER
stands by the pile of baggage.

NIKOLAI. Beneš and the rest of his political rabbits have
formed a government in Kosice. (*He smiles at* SIMON.)
But Communists have all the key ministries.

Pause.

SIMON. I haven't exactly been keeping up with things, Nikolai.
(*Pause.*) I was never very political, you know. (*Pause.*)
Byzantium. That was my little corner. (*Pause.*) What's your
little corner nowadays?

Pause.

NIKOLAI (*smiling*). I'm a rat-catcher.

SIMON. Er — Russian rats?

NIKOLAI. I'm an internationalist.

SIMON *takes a long pull of the vodka, and leans back against
the seat holding up the canteen.*

SIMON. What I've always liked about you fellows (*belches*) is
your absolute impartiality. (*Pause.*) That noble concept:
impartiality. (*Pause.*) What it means in Russia of course, is
that no one is safe from you at all. (*Pause.*) But don't let's
bicker, Nikolai. Shall we not bicker? (*Pause.*) I do believe
I hear music! The Nazi beast has fled — leaving behind a
gramophone which is even now being pumped by some
sturdy peasant. (*Pause.*) How charming! (*He drinks again.*)
After the smoke and stench of battle —

And indeed we can hear the sound of BLANKA's *gramophone.
Even* NIKOLAI *is involuntarily caught by it.* SIMON *waves
his bottle.*

SIMON. Some sturdy peasant —

12. Interior. Country house. Kitchen. Afternoon. MILENA *is furiously cleaning up the mess. She stops suddenly, with the feeling of being watched.*

NIKOLAI *stands in the doorway to the corridor. Behind him,* SIMON *and the* DRIVER. MILENA *glares at him.*

NIKOLAI. Do you speak Russian?

MILENA (*dryly*). Mother of God, it's the Red Army! (*She approaches him, hands on hips.*) Requisition, rape, or just passing through?

NIKOLAI *steps into the room taking a document from his breast pocket.* SIMON *sidles in beside him.*

NIKOLAI. This is the house (*looking at the document*) of Bohumil and . . . Francesca Soltesz?

Pause.

MILENA. Dead. (*Pause.*) Both of them.

NIKOLAI. The Germans?

MILENA. Yes. He was taken in nineteen forty-two. His ashes were returned by the Germans in nineteen forty-three in a cardboard box. (*Pause.*) Madam Francesca died six months later.

NIKOLAI. The Germans requisitioned this house?

MILENA. In nineteen forty-one.

Pause.

NIKOLAI. The factory in the village?

MILENA. The Germans — being German — took Mr Soltesz under escort to Vienna in nineteen forty-one, and made him sign over the factory what they called 'legally'. (*Pause.*) There's a daughter. Blanka. I took her away after her mother's death. We got here just two days ago. They'd left behind some men to burn papers and shoot the guard dogs. We hid in that bunker in front of the house.

NIKOLAI. *You* took Blanka Soltesz away?

MILENA. I'm her nurse. I suppose I should say I *was* her nurse when she was a child. God knows what I am now. (*Pause.*) I think she's a bit crazy. (*Pause.*) I've tried to protect her. I think she —

NIKOLAI. Where is she?

MILENA. Playing waltz records in the old ballroom. (*Pause.*) Are you lot going to take the house now?

NIKOLAI. I'm here to decide that. Among other things. (*He straightens up.*) Colonel Nikolai Shchetkin.

MILENA *is staring at* SIMON, *who has propped himself against a wall, staring dreamily through the open door to the kitchen garden.*

MILENA. Who's the fat one?

NIKOLAI *joins her in staring at* SIMON, *who is unconsciously feeling his stomach and consciously resenting being called fat.*

NIKOLAI. Rusakov. You're a cook — cook something.

He goes out. The DRIVER *starts bringing the wine, the pig and the vegetables into the kitchen.*
MILENA *and* SIMON *eye each other warily. He reaches for a chair and slumps into it.*

SIMON. I am not fat.

MILENA. You're not starving.

SIMON. Ah well. We liberators, you know. We live off the fat of the land. Can I take my boots off?

MILENA (*as he pulls off his boots*). Liberators! *You?*

SIMON. All the way from Moscow. Semyon Vasilievich Rusakov, Madam. Definitely not at your service. (*He holds up the canteen, which he has been hiding.*) A little vodka?

MILENA *finds two glasses and bangs them down in front of him.*
The DRIVER *has stopped to take notice, and she gets a third glass.*
SIMON *puts a little vodka in two of the glasses and fills the third, which he drinks at once. The others follow suit.*
SIMON *fills his own glass again. The* DRIVER *goes out.*

SIMON (*drinking*). If only I could get really drunk and stay that way for ever!

MILENA. I'm an educated woman, you know.

SIMON. I don't quite see what that — ?

MILENA. No one's going to treat me like a servant.

SIMON. Er — we are supposed to be *communists*, you know.

MILENA. Rubbish!

SIMON. Well I don't say *I'm* a communist. (*He stretches in his chair, holding up his glass and squinting at it.*) More a bit of an outcast, you might say. A dud. A failure. A natural-born sheep, driven to live out his days in a somewhat foxy manner. If I am a slave to anything, Madam — it is to the weary consolation of empty rhetoric. (*He finishes his drink and pours another, emptying the canteen.*) My mother intended me for a priest. Nature for a poet. (*Drinking.*) And the Revolution? I have no idea what the Revolution intended me for. (*He brandishes the glass.*) Revolution is for turning underdogs into overdogs, d'you see? And brands the natural aristocrats of this world as mere curs!

MILENA. Mister — is it Lieutenant? — Rusakov. If you're a natural anything — it's a natural fool!

SIMON. How true, how true!

MILENA. Are you a cook or aren't you? And if you are — can you do it drunk?

SIMON — *exhausted and really quite drunk by now — leans towards her, wagging a finger.*

SIMON. That Colonel Shchetkin. He was once a pupil of mine. Can you believe it? (*He cups his chin in his hand gazing into* MILENA's *eyes.*) One of what I used to call our 'poster people'.

MILENA. Meaning!

SIMON. Didn't you ever see our Soviet posters in the thirties? Girls, and tractors . . . sheaves of wheat . . . workers marching with clenched fists into the Soviet utopia? (*Pause.*) Well I always thought . . . ten years ago that is . . . that young Shchetkin looked as if he'd just stepped down from one of those posters. (*He looks round the kitchen.*) Isn't the local drink something miraculously potent called slivovic? I wonder if those Nazi buggers left any behind?

MILENA. You're drunk enough already!

SIMON. Can one ever *be* drunk enough? I doubt if you could find me a single Russian who would think so. (*He is suddenly aghast at himself.*) Good God! It only takes a few glasses the morning after, and one takes off again like a bloody rocket! (*Pause.*) I shall be weeping, in a minute. I know the signs. (*He totters to his feet.*) Nothing but a windy coward, spewing words to hide the dark void of the soul. (*He raises both hands towards the ceiling.*) The dark soul of Mother Russia!

He falls flat on his face and begins to snore at once.

13. Interior. Country house. Hall. Afternoon. NIKOLAI *is running briskly down a wide staircase which rises in a majestic sweep from the hall. At the foot of the stairs he stands and listens. We hear another waltz beginning.*

14. Interior. Country house. Ballroom. Afternoon. *The gramophone is playing.* BLANKA *sits on the floor beside it, her knees pulled up to her chin, her face pressed into her folded arms.*

NIKOLAI *appears soundlessly in the ballroom entrance.*

The needle sticks on the gramophone. As BLANKA *turns to fix it, she sees* NIKOLAI — *who slowly walks down the ballroom towards her. She stops the gramophone, rising.*

NIKOLAI. Blanka Soltesz?

Pause.

BLANKA. Yes.

NIKOLAI. Colonel Nikolai Shchetkin.

Pause.

BLANKA. Yes?

Pause.

NIKOLAI (*uncertainly*). What a magnificent room!

BLANKA. Is the war over, Colonel Shchetkin?

NIKOLAI. For you it is.

Pause.

BLANKA. What are you doing in this house?

Pause.

NIKOLAI. I think we would like to use it for a little while.

BLANKA. We?

NIKOLAI. The Red Army. (*Pause.*) My . . . unit . . . needs a temporary headquarters.

Pause.

BLANKA. Where is Doctor Beneš?

NIKOLAI. In Kosice. (*Pause.*) With his Provisional Government.

BLANKA. And Mr Masaryk?

NIKOLAI. Why do you ask?

BLANKA. My father knew Mr Masaryk. (*Pause.*) We all loved him.

Pause.

NIKOLAI. I believe Masaryk is the Minister of Foreign Affairs.

Pause.

BLANKA. So — we are free?

NIKOLAI *crosses to one of the tall windows and looks out.*

NIKOLAI. You spent your childhood here? In this house?

BLANKA. It seems very dreamlike now.

Pause.

NIKOLAI. So does my own childhood in Kiev. (*Pause.*) But then I went to Moscow. (*He turns to her smiling.*) I wanted to be an archaeologist. (*Pause.*) That old woman in the kitchen —

BLANKA. Milena? She's not so old.

NIKOLAI. She looks like a peasant. But then when she speaks — (BLANKA *is laughing — almost giggling.* NIKOLAI's *face hardens.*) Yes?

BLANKA. Was she rude to you?

Pause.

NIKOLAI. Do you know why the Germans took your father?

BLANKA. Isn't that an absurd question? They took anyone who . . . who —

NIKOLAI. Who what?

BLANKA *is in a sudden rage, and stamps her foot.*

BLANKA. You are so *stupid!*

Pause.

NIKOLAI. And I've no doubt you are a spoiled silly child.
(*Pause.*) Brought up to what? Vanity and privilege. (*Pause.*)
And then one day — the Nazis arrive!

BLANKA. And now they've gone. And my parents are dead. And
this is *my* house.

NIKOLAI. Spoiled, silly — and ignorant.

*NIKOLAI laughs suddenly, reaching out a hand to touch
her lightly on the cheek. She slaps it away. He recoils, angry.*

NIKOLAI. You will instruct that old woman to clean and
prepare a room for me. Tomorrow she can make a start on
the rest of the house. My driver will help her. (*Grimly.*)
You might even try a little dirty work yourself.

*He turns away on his heel, making for the door. He stops as
BLANKA shrills out:*

BLANKA. One doesn't *instruct* Milena. Not about anything. She's
not a servant.

NIKOLAI (*turning*). If you don't, I will.

*Sulkily she kneels on the floor and starts the waltz record
again. NIKOLAI stands watching her for the first few bars,
then walks away.*

BLANKA. Colonel Shchetkin — (*Pause, as he hesitates.*)
Colonel Shchetkin — will you dance with me?

*She approaches him and stands close, innocently provocative.
He raises his arms and they begin to dance, NIKOLAI very
stiff and formal, the victim of a situation which he is
completely unable to categorise.*
    *We follow them dancing — dreamlike, and very slightly
comical.*

15. Exterior. Country road. Dusk. *A rough, horse-drawn cart
is grinding along the road slowly.*
    *At the front, a PEASANT dozes. At the back, on a pile of
potatoes, the RUSSIAN SOLDIER and his bicycle from Scene
3. He is fast asleep, tangled up with the bicycle. The wristwatches
on his arms gleam in the failing light.*

16. Exterior. Country house. Night. *Several windows are blazing
with light.*

17. Interior. Country house. Bedroom. Night. *Moonlight.*
BLANKA *sleeps in a huge four-poster bed, clutching a cardboard
box to her stomach. We glimpse a tapestried wall, a pile of rubbish
in one corner, an escritoire by the window. On a couch opposite
the bed,* MILENA *is asleep, in her long black peasant dress.*
BLANKA *moans quietly in her sleep.*

18. Interior. Country house. Bedroom. Night. *A room similar
to* BLANKA's, *but with an ordinary double bed.*
   NIKOLAI *sits at a table writing in the circle of light from a
desk-lamp. There are piles of documents by his elbow. On the
floor, the three tin boxes we saw in the jeep — one of them
open. He stops writing and wearily rubs his eyes, runs his hands
through his short hair. He lights a cigarette and leans back in his
chair, his eyes closed.*
   Somewhere outside a dog is barking petulantly.

19. Interior. Country house. Kitchen. Night. *The kitchen is
transformed from how we saw it before: clean, scrubbed, rows
of metal pots and pans gleaming along one wall.*
   At the table: SIMON *and the* DRIVER *are playing cards, with
a bottle between them.*
   *A radio on the table is broadcasting in Czech (perhaps a
section from the 'Kosice Programme' — 'the programme opened
with a government tribute to the Soviet Union and a pledge to
support the Red Army until final victory. For this purpose the
government announced the formation of a new Czechoslovak
army, trained, organised and equipped on the model of the
Red Army.').*
   The DRIVER *irritably switches off the radio.*

DRIVER. D'you get the drift of it?

SIMON. Here and there.

   The DRIVER *plays a card and fills their glasses.*

DRIVER. By God you can drink! I will say —

SIMON. How else to unite the scattered fragments of the soul?
   Drinking to me is a kind of research, Comrade Brodovich.
   Psychological research. (*Pause.*) With most men it's a brutish
   business. But in the case of Semyon Vasilievich, as the Colonel
   is prone to address me — vodka is the mirror of the heart.

BRODOVICH. What a clown!

SIMON. A clown? Ah well. In the plays of Shakespeare . . . clowns, you know —

BRODOVICH. Thank God there's a new generation coming up!

SIMON. You're quite right. The Revolution can do without people like me. (*Pause.*) Those who stand on the spiritual heights, Brodovich. Lifting their careworn faces to the stars —

BRODOVICH. Just one more snivelling, bombastic professor!

SIMON. Do you despise the life of the mind?

BRODOVICH. I despise bullshit.

SIMON *eyes him benignly and empties his glass.*

SIMON. This slivovic isn't bad at all, is it? (*Smacks his lips.*) The bouquet. (*Smacks his lips.*) Something — would you say? — between rusty nails and dog's vomit?

BRODOVICH *throws his cards down irritably, then sweeps both them and* SIMON's *cards off the table. He refills his glass and drains it.*

BRODOVICH. Did you see the girl?

Pause.

SIMON. Girl?

BRODOVICH. In that big room at the front —

SIMON *belches, and speaks with a German accent:*

SIMON. Ze ballroom?

BRODOVICH. Dancing to a gramophone. On and on and on. Dancing.

Pause.

SIMON (*dreamily*). I glimpsed an angel, for a moment. (*Pause.*) I was crawling about on all fours looking for a lavatory. (*Pause.*) An angel. Brodovich. Not dancing. Floating. (*Pause.*) One looked. One adored. One reluctantly withdrew with an aching bladder. (*Pause.*) I wonder what Colonel Nikolai Shchetkin has in mind for me? (*Pause.*) I feel like the mouse that the cat paralyses with a quick bite in the spine, then drops in a corner. (*Pause.*) Something to relieve life's huge boredom later on. (*Pause.*) Yes. Shchetkin is feline. I've been racking my scrambled brains for the word.

BRODOVICH. Well. How long is it since *you* had a woman?

SIMON (*smiling benignly*). Proletarian cur! (*Pause.*) Shoo!
Foof! Desecrate not these poor old hairy ears.

Pause.

BRODOVICH. What about the spoils of war? Eh?

Pause.

SIMON. The phrase has an antique ring, Brodovich. I take it
you mean rape? (*Pause.*) Primitive boy! Notice your
disrespect for women. Notice how you speak of 'having' them.
You give the impression of an entire Russian horde compressed
into the itching body of a single half-baked kolkhoznik!
(*Drinking.*) Fie on you! (*Pause.*) Mind you. In my time. Years
ago. I did have a fat cow of mine own. (*Pause.*) My very own.
(*Pause.*) She married me because I had a whole room to
myself. (*Pause.*) A *whole room*, Brodovich. And in Moscow,
too. (*Pause.*) Can you imagine the sense of space . . . of high
living? (*Pause.*) Then she denounced me. She got the room
and I got ten years. Happily, if mistakenly, commuted to
three later on. (*Pause.*) That was the way ladies went about
things in those days, Brodovich.

Pause.

BRODOVICH. About this girl —

SIMON. I can't help it . . . I am consumed . . . with anxiety . . .
for my skin.

Pause.

BRODOVICH. Shchetkin'll have her.

SIMON (*barking*). Oh no he won't!

There is a long silence. BRODOVICH *is grinning.* SIMON *is
startled by his own vehemence.*

BRODOVICH (*leering*). You're past it — aren't you?

SIMON (*haughtily*). I am not in need of it.

BRODOVICH. What is it? Your prostate?

SIMON. There are men — I am possibly the first you have
encountered — who are fastidious.

BRODOVICH. That's right. Prostatitis.

SIMON lurches to his feet, clutching his glass.

SIMON. Comrade Brodovich — do not provoke me. I have no
reserves of violence to bluster with. (*He teeters over*
BRODOVICH.) My wounds are not in the balls, but in the
soul.

BRODOVICH (*nastily*). The soul of Mother Russia!

SIMON *waves his arms upwards, and in a singsong bawl:*

SIMON. Correct, dumb peasant! The soul of Mother Russia!

And falls flat on his face on the floor.
BRODOVICH *scrapes his chair round to contemplate the
snoring body. As he lifts his glass, he sees* NIKOLAI *in the
doorway, in shirtsleeves and affectedly holding a cigarette.*

NIKOLAI. I wonder what Chekhov would have made of *him?*

20. Exterior. Country road. Dawn. *The horse and cart of
Scene 15 are drawn up by the roadside. The* RUSSIAN SOLDIER
*stands in the road, pulling down his bicycle in a shower of
potatoes. The sun has barely lifted over the horizon. The*
PEASANT DRIVER *watches the* RUSSIAN, *then cracks his
whip. The old horse strains at the cart. As it moves off:*

PEASANT DRIVER. Hey —

The RUSSIAN SOLDIER *stands gaping at him, and the* OLD
MAN *throws a dark green bottle which the* SOLDIER *expertly
catches. The cart creaks off down the road, and the* RUSSIAN
*(they are at a crossroads) peers up at a roadsign in Czech.
He drinks, pulling the cork out of the bottle with his teeth.
He listens to the wristwatches on both arms. Drinks again.
Climbs onto the bicycle and pedals a zigzag course back the
way they have come.*

21. Interior. Country house. Bathroom. Morning. *The bathroom
joins* NIKOLAI's *bedroom, which we can see through the half-
open door.* NIKOLAI *is shaving, stripped to the waist.* BLANKA
*appears in the doorway and stands looking at his naked back.
This morning she is dressed in a neat print dress, her long hair
caught in a clasp at the nape of her neck. She looks cool and
dignified, a little older than yesterday, and not at all wild. She is
acting.*

BLANKA. I'm sorry there is no hot water. (*Pause.*) Yet.

NIKOLAI. Good morning! (*He turns to look at her.*) I got some from the kitchen.

BLANKA. *You* did?

NIKOLAI. Why not?

Pause.

BLANKA. Why not that young man you have with you?

NIKOLAI (*laughing*). He's my driver.

Pause.

BLANKA. The telephone doesn't work yet, either.

NIKOLAI. It will. Some time today probably.

Pause.

BLANKA. Will peace be declared? Or signed? Or what? (*Pause.*) How do they do it?

NIKOLAI. There'll be a formal surrender.

BLANKA. And Hitler?

NIKOLAI. I'm sure he won't let himself be taken alive.

BLANKA. And the others?

NIKOLAI. The Soviet Union and her Allies will try them.

BLANKA. You wouldn't think it needed a trial. I hope they shoot them all.

Pause.

NIKOLAI. So do I.

Pause.

BLANKA. Who's the unhappy-looking soldier you have with you? The middle-aged man. With his hair sticking up in spikes. (*Pause.*) He has a most peculiar manner.

NIKOLAI. Haven't you ever seen a man shave before?

BLANKA. Who is he?

NIKOLAI. Just an old friend I picked up drunk in a ditch. About thirty kilometres from here.

BLANKA. But he *is* an officer?

NIKOLAI (*smiling*). A *kind* of officer.

BLANKA. That's all right then. Because I invited him to breakfast with you and me on the terrace.

Pause.

NIKOLAI. You did — *what?*

BLANKA. Before the war, we often had breakfast on the terrace in fine weather. Mother and Father. And me. And Milena. (*Pause.*) And guests, more often than not. (*Pause.*) Don't you think one should resume civilised habits as soon as possible?

She is very grave. NIKOLAI is trying hard not to laugh. He swills his face and reaches for a towel.

NIKOLAI. Oh yes! Civilised habits. (*But he can't resist jabbing.*) You people must have found the war a tiresome interruption.

BLANKA. They killed my father. And my mother died because of that. She was too unhappy to live without him, can't you understand?

Pause.

NIKOLAI. I'm sorry, Blanka —

Pause.

BLANKA. On the terrace, then. In ten minutes. (*Pause.*) It's a little fresh, being April. And we only have bread and tea. But the sky's blue. (*Pause.*) It was lovely yesterday. A gift from God.

He watches her go out through the bedroom door, then slowly resumes towelling his face.

22. Exterior. Country house. Terrace. Morning. *A wide terrace with a stone balustrade, overlooking the countryside. There are tall french windows giving access to what must have been a breakfast room, but has been used by the Germans as an office. The long table on the terrace is a bizarre sight, in the circumstances: a white cloth, delicate china, silver, sparkling glasses, enough for a ritual breakfast of several courses. On a side table: a large silver teapot and hot water jug, and a long dish with a neat row of slices of rough black bread.*
　　BLANKA is arranging roses in a bowl on the table as MILENA comes out from the breakfast room. She looks pityingly at the table and at BLANKA.

MILENA. Roses? For *Russians?*

BLANKA (*happily*). The Germans had looked after the hot-houses. I went to see this morning. (*Pause.*) I expect they liked the peaches.

MILENA. Oh, I'm sure they did!

SIMON *comes onto the terrace. He has made an effort, though his uniform is very crumpled, enveloping him like a sagging concertina. However, he has shaved and polished his rimless glasses, combed his hair, cleaned his fingernails. He hovers uncertainly, half bowing several times, wary of* MILENA.

SIMON. Semyon Vasilievich Rusakov. At the service of humanity, freedom and justice. Byzantine history a lifelong passion. Melancholy. Passive. A disgusting urge to wag his tail and please everyone. (*He sniffs the air.*) Real tea?

MILENA. Hungover, are we? You seem a bit excitable.

SIMON. I often find, Madam — that a shave in really hot water disperses those other fumes. In this case, last night's slivovic. A truly abominable potion. But on it one climbs — if one may speak of climbing a liquid — unto the peaks, the pinnacles. Humble man, repressed as he is into the bargain — strives for a little beatitude.

MILENA (*to* BLANKA). There you are you see. I told you he was a professor. One of those that make up for empty heads with a pitiable gush of words.

SIMON. What a neat turn of phrase you have yourself, Miss Milena. (*Flopping into a chair.*) Where *would* we all have been without the Treaty of Versailles?

BLANKA. Lieutenant Rusakov —

SIMON. Simon if you please, Miss Soltesz. The commission is notional, for cooks. And I always insisted on informality with my students. (*Pause.*) I thought Lenin would have approved.

He is staring at the plate of bread. BLANKA *follows his glance.*

BLANKA. We must wait for Colonel Shchetkin.

SIMON. I would do *anything* to ingratiate myself with Colonel Shchetkin. Were he an octopus, I'd lick each of his eight boots from morning till night. I am the New Soviet Man, young lady. A Stakhanovite of the survival problem.

MILENA. He can even gibber at this hour of the morning!

BLANKA. I really don't understand what you are talking about — Simon.

SIMON. The great thing about modern warfare — so mobile, so uncompromising — is that here and there, you find small pockets of territory which somehow get by-passed by the unheeding juggernaut itself. (*Pause.*) How fortunate we are to enjoy one such . . . one such small *pocket*. (*He pulls at his jacket.*) It's none too warm, of course. But —

MILENA *starts to pour him a cup of tea.*

BLANKA. Breakfast in *ten minutes*, I told Colonel Shchetkin.

SIMON (*bleakly*). Al fresco — (MILENA *thrusts the cup of tea at him, which he clutches gratefully and drinks.*) Punctuality. Yes. Well. We Russians — (*finishes his tea.*) Have you ground your way through a page or two of our literature, Miss Soltesz?

BLANKA. Blanka.

SIMON. Pushkin? Lermontov? (*Pause.*) The unquenchable Gorky? (*Pause.*) Blanka?

BLANKA. Well of course. I had a Russian governess.

SIMON. A poor exile? A piece of flotsam washed out of our country by the Bolshevik tide?

MILENA (*tartly*). Born and bred in Berlin.

SIMON. Believe me, I didn't mean to take off like that. (*Holds out his cup.*) Such a romantic!

MILENA *lets him go on holding the cup. He replaces it with exaggerated precision on the table. He beams at* BLANKA.

SIMON. May I say how lovely you look this morning? How fresh? (*Pause.*) One tries to have simple reactions. And the rhetorical mood, you know — even I can't keep it up.

Pause.

BLANKA. Thank you.

She is sitting imperiously at the table. She drums her fingers on the cloth.

SIMON (*absently*). And so young, I imagine.

BLANKA. No. (*Pause.*) I'm eighteen.

SIMON. Ah, yes! (*Pause.*) Quite mature. Do forgive me. (*Pause.*) But young, I meant — to be Shchetkin-ed. (*Pause.*) You crawl out of your bunker one morning. Miss Milena here told me. And before you know where you are — Shchetkin-ed. (*Pause.*) It is cruel. (*Pause.*) I had the same experience in an otherwise rather hospitable ditch.

Pause.

BLANKA. Are you two gentlemen *enemies?*

SIMON. Haven't you noticed his cap?

MILENA. Now just you wait a minute —

SIMON *obediently presses his lips together, drawing one forefinger across them.* BLANKA *is looking from one to the other.*

BLANKA. What does *he* mean?

MILENA (*gently*). Nothing at all, my love.

BLANKA *bangs her fist on the table, glaring at* SIMON.

BLANKA. What do you *mean?*

Pause.

SIMON. N.K.V.D. (*Pause.*) Since you're eighteen. (*Snapping at* MILENA.) Don't be a fool, woman!

BLANKA. And don't you be rude to her.

SIMON *lowers his head to the table.*

SIMON. I grovel. I grovel. (NIKOLAI *comes onto the terrace.* SIMON, *his cheek pressed to the table, stares up innocently and puts his tongue out.*) I grovel.

NIKOLAI. By all means. Anything that comes naturally to you. (*To* BLANKA.) May I sit down? (*He sits down, noticing the roses.*) What beautiful roses!

SIMON (*straightening up*). And in April too.

MILENA *is pouring tea and passing round the bread.* SIMON *sits chewing abstractedly.* NIKOLAI *takes something from his pocket and holds it out to* BLANKA, *hidden in his fist.*

MILENA. Those Nazis! They didn't leave much. A little tea.
A few maggoty bones —

BLANKA. What is it?

NIKOLAI. Hold your hand out —

*She does so. He opens his hand on her palm — a small,
wizened lemon.*

BLANKA. A *lemon!* I haven't seen one for — (*She presses it to
her nose, smelling.*) Look, Milena —

SIMON (*glumly*). It's very poetic. Whoever thought the day
would come when lemons would grow on security officers?
(*Pause.*) Whatever will he sprout next?

BLANKA. Slice it up, Milena. And we'll have some. (*Pause.*)
Tea with lemon!

MILENA *takes the lemon as if it were a grenade. She holds it
up between thumb and forefinger.*

MILENA. There's less juice in this poor lemon than there is in
Comrade Rusakov. (*Pause.*) All the way from where, Colonel?

NIKOLAI. Georgia.

SIMON. Ah, Georgia! The mountains. The shashlik —

MILENA *takes the lemon to the side table and slices it
carefully laying the pieces on a saucer which she then passes
round. They all put a slice in their tea, except SIMON, who
chews his.*

BLANKA. Thank you *very much*, Colonel Shchetkin.

SIMON. I'll bet General Eisenhower has lemon in his tea *every*
morning. (*Pause.*) How civilised this table looks! Such trouble
you must have gone to, dear young lady. For two weary
soldiers, still reeking of cordite. Still reeling from the terrible
sound of Armageddon.

NIKOLAI. Semyon Vasilievich —

SIMON. Yass?

NIKOLAI. Shut up.

MILENA. Not even a bit of ersatz margarine —

SIMON *plants his elbows on the table, folds his face in his
hands and closes his eyes. The others drink their tea
(MILENA sitting by the side table) and eat their bread.*

NIKOLAI *and* BLANKA *are looking at each other. She lowers her eyes, blushing. It is a timeless moment — the ludicrously formal table, the roses, the countryside beyond the terrace.*

SIMON's *elbow slips off the table and he falls off his chair. Lying surprised and jolted, to peals of laughter from* BLANKA, SIMON *sees a cardboard box under the table near her feet. Hauls himself back onto his chair.* BLANKA *puts her hand to her mouth and straightens her face.*

BLANKA. Before the war, we used to sit at breakfast and plan the day. (*Pause.*) Of course my father usually went to his factory. (*Pause.*) You know, Colonel Shchetkin. He built houses for his workers. And a sports-ground. A swimming pool. A club. A clinic. (*Pause.*) The workers had shares in the factory. It was a model enterprise. (*Pause.*) I don't think there was anything quite like it, anywhere in Czechoslovakia. (*Pause: then firmly.*) *Everyone* said what a progressive man he was.

Pause.

NIKOLAI. And what did the factory produce?

BLANKA. Irrigation equipment. Very *advanced* irrigation equipment. (*Pause.*) Quite ahead of its time.

Pause.

SIMON. What's in that cardboard box under the table?

We see MILENA *stiffen.* BLANKA *carries on as if she hadn't heard.*

BLANKA. I shall make this house exactly as it used to be. (*Pause.*) My father was wealthy. So *I* must be wealthy. (*Pause.*) He said wealth is not immoral in itself. It depends on how it is used. (*Pause.*) There used to be such lovely balls. We'd have a band from Prague. And lanterns in the trees. (*Pause.*) I neither know nor understand the Soviet Union, Colonel Shchetkin. But life here was — gracious. Yes. That's the word.

Pause.

NIKOLAI. Through the eyes of a child.

Pause.

BLANKA. Wasn't it, Milena?

MILENA. It certainly was, my dear.

BLANKA. There you are, you see! Milena wasn't a child.
(*Pause.*) But. (*Pause.*) I don't know what *you* intend, Colonel
Shchetkin.

Pause.

NIKOLAI. I sincerely hope we shall not inconvenience you.

SIMON. How one does yearn — absolutely *yearn* — for the
gracious life! I remember in nineteen twelve —

NIKOLAI (*cutting in*). But war doesn't end just like a broken
nightmare. (*He turns to* MILENA.) Where *have* you two
been since the Germans moved in here?

MILENA. We managed to get away with Madam Soltesz.
To my mother's house in a small village about twenty-five
kilometres away. (*Pause.*) When Madam died, we stayed there.
It was out of the way. (*Pause.*) You should be honest with
us, Colonel Shchetkin. (*Pause.*) She deserves your respect.

SIMON *breaks into a fit of uncontrollable laughter at the*
word 'respect'. NIKOLAI *slaps his face hard. There is a long*
silence. BLANKA *takes the box from under the table and*
runs into the house. MILENA *follows her. There are tears*
running down SIMON's *cheeks.*

SIMON. But you respect no one, Nikolai. Do you? (*He stands*
over NIKOLAI, *trembling.*) And we are not permitted to
respect ourselves, either. (*Pause.*) The weak are either crushed,
or become fawning caricatures of human beings. The strong —
well look at you, Comrade Shchetkin! Ten years haven't
changed you, either. How well I remember you as a student!
Watch him, watch him, I said to myself!

NIKOLAI. Do you think I'm strong, then?

SIMON. You have what counts for strength. (*He is recovering*
his balance.) You have your bit of power. And I suppose
you've rearranged any decent values you might once have
sincerely held. (*Dryly.*) In the name of that higher morality
we call self-interest.

Pause.

NIKOLAI. Were you running away, Simon?

Pause.

SIMON. I don't know.

Pause.

NIKOLAI. Whom do you despise most? Me or you?

Pause.

SIMON. Myself. (*Pause.*) Yes.

Pause.

NIKOLAI. I can have you shot, you realise? You know what you are — objectively.

SIMON. I wonder how many poor Russian heads ache with the clang of that word *objectively!* (*Pause.*) Do firing-squads use subjective or objective bullets? (*Pause.*) And by the way. Am I dreaming this house? You? That girl? The peculiar absence of the war from these parts? (*Pause.*) Am I still mercifully in my ditch, full of vodka? (*Pause.*) What's going on? Or should I say why *isn't* anything going on?

NIKOLAI. Patience, patience —

SIMON. I mean. If there were a few mountains we could be in Switzerland! (*Pause.*) If only we were!

NIKOLAI. A nice little apartment in Zurich? Growing old gently, far away from the moral and intellectual squalor of life in Moscow? (*Pause.*) Yes. One is already beginning to anticipate life after the war. It's very human. (*He has become distant, inward.*) I'm sorry I slapped you. Truly ashamed of myself.

He exits quickly through the adjoining room. MILENA comes onto the terrace as SIMON sits down deep in thought. She bangs and clatters around the table, clearing BLANKA's pathetic demonstration of 'graciousness'.

23. Interior. Country house. Bedroom. Morning. BLANKA's *room. She stands by the window looking out. On the escritoire in front of her the cardboard box. It is tied with string, and she is absently plucking at the thick knot in the centre as she gazes through the window.*
From BLANKA's *point of view:*

24. Exterior. Country house. Day. *The* RUSSIAN SOLDIER *on his bicycle comes wobbling up the drive towards the house. In*

*front of it, he falls off. One wheel is spinning, and he watches it
bemusedly as he drinks from the bottle given to him by the*
PEASANT. *He climbs back on the bicycle and rides off down the
other side of the drive.*

25. Interior. Country house bedroom. Morning. *There is a
knock at the door.* BLANKA *turns from the window.*

BLANKA. Come in.

   NIKOLAI *enters. He goes towards her, but stops in the middle
   of the room.*

NIKOLAI. You are upset. (*Pause.*) I'm sorry.

BLANKA. You humiliated him.

   Pause.

NIKOLAI. I apologised to him.

BLANKA. It was true what Milena said. You *should* respect me.

   Pause.

NIKOLAI. I do. I assure you.

BLANKA. I don't think Lieutenant Rusakov was being cynical.

NIKOLAI. Oh yes he was.

BLANKA. Unjustly?

   Pause.

NIKOLAI. The Rusakovs always wallow in their sense of having
   been abused by life. (*He sits wearily on the bed.*) Do I have to
   defend myself on the subject of Rusakov?

BLANKA. Well *I* like him.

NIKOLAI. He's a one-man comedy. Very nearly a farce.

BLANKA. Then that's his tragedy — isn't it?

NIKOLAI. Is there such a thing as a *just* cynicism?

BLANKA. I expect I meant justifiable.

   Pause.

NIKOLAI. Is he worth so much scrupulous concern?

BLANKA. Isn't everyone?

NIKOLAI. Including those Nazi war criminals you hope will be shot?

Pause.

BLANKA. Go away, please.

NIKOLAI *(rising)*. Well. I was going for a walk.

BLANKA. You don't seem to have anything to do here. Why don't you go away and leave us?

Pause.

NIKOLAI. In a few hours I shall be — militarily speaking — in the same predicament as Rusakov. *(Pause.)* I mean, I *could* be.

BLANKA. Aren't you supposed to be here?

NIKOLAI. Oh, yes! *(Pause.)* But I have certain orders, too

Pause.

BLANKA. Simon is a deserter?

NIKOLAI. Technically. He certainly isn't where he should be. *(Pause.)* I *have* been playing with him a little. *(He grins.)* I'll get him out of it somehow. *(Pause.)* He was as ineffectual a professor as he is a soldier. We used to make fun of him at the university. Then. Well sometimes the habit coarsens. And you begin to make people squirm. You rationalise your satisfaction in their misery. As if it's not because someone is weak, or foolish, or naive. But because they deserve to suffer. Or invite it.

BLANKA. Why was he funny in the first place. He isn't stupid. And he mocks himself all the time. What made you all pick on him? Was he a bad teacher?

NIKOLAI. He was a good teacher. At any rate a good historian. And articulate. But he lost his way in his own theories. We wanted to know what he thought about the Revolution — about what we were doing in Russia. *(Pause.)* That used to make his eyes glaze over, I can tell you.

Pause.

BLANKA. But there's some personal antagonism between you and him.

Pause.

NIKOLAI. He never troubled to understand what was going on. He was incorrigibly bourgeois. He rubbed everyone up the wrong way, with his lofty principles and pedantic moralising. (*Pause.*) We thought him squeamish. He said he was proud to be thought squeamish by Marxists. (*Pause.*) Ach! It's all ten years ago. I can't be bothered. (*He crosses to her and puts his hands on her shoulders: she looks from one hand to the other, not moving.*) I don't want to defend myself by criticising Rusakov.

She disengages herself — gently, abstractedly. Once more she slips into another mental dimension — a kind of 'absence' from here and now.

BLANKA. We shall be dining in the ballroom tonight. (*Pause.*) Will you ask Simon if he'll clean the chandelier? It's filthy. And when it's clean and lit up, it's like a huge cluster of diamonds.

NIKOLAI. *Dining?* (*Pause.*) Clean the *chandelier?*

BLANKA. Milena said you brought some wine. (*Pause.*) We can't dine in the dining room. Have you seen it? It's a worse mess than the rest of the house. (*Pause.*) There's . . . there's dried excrement on the floor. And brown stains everywhere. (*Pause.*) I think one should distinguish carefully between the Wehrmacht — and the Gestapo. Don't you? The Wehrmacht was always — most correct.

She takes the cardboard box and goes to the bed, where she sits with it on her knees, rocking backwards and forwards.
    NIKOLAI *is chilled.*

NIKOLAI. Were you ever — personally hurt by the Germans, Blanka?

Pause.

BLANKA. Personally?

Pause.

NIKOLAI. Physically.

Pause.

BLANKA. Oh no. (*Pause.*) Oh no.

Pause.

NIKOLAI. I have to make an inspection of the grounds. Will you come with me?

BLANKA. I keep having the strangest sensations. My mind blurs.
I don't feel as if the last five years have happened at all.
(*Pause.*) But then I only have to look around me, don't I?
(*Pause.*) I keep imagining myself eighteen without the war.
(*Pause.*) I don't hallucinate. But I keep almost hearing and
seeing another life. Music. Voices. People laughing. (*Pause.*)
I smell fresh cherries everywhere in this house. (*Pause.*)
Of course, it's my father's death, isn't it? I have such a vivid
memory of him feeding me cherries. On the terrace where
we had breakfast. (*Pause.*) When I saw the roses in the
hothouse this morning, I wasn't surprised at all. They're a
special kind that Mother was — what did she call it? —
hybridising? (*Pause.*) I was so delighted, I could have eaten
them. (*Pause. Smiling.*) Can you imagine a Nazi officer
hybridising? (*Pause.*) My sense of where and when I am keeps
jumping about. (*Pause.*) Nothing's changed for me since
my parents died. I haven't grown. I've aged five years without
developing. There was nothing at all in Milena's village for a
child like me. Nothing. They were dumb, grim people.
Prejudiced and superstitious. Catholic peasants with ancient
wooden heads. I used to hide in the woods and scream till
my throat was sore.

She goes into a reverie. NIKOLAI *touches her cheek gently.*

NIKOLAI. Come with me —

BLANKA. And what I said about tonight?

NIKOLAI. It — embarrasses me.

BLANKA. Childish games!

NIKOLAI. You must do as you wish.

BLANKA. I embarrass myself.

Pause.

NIKOLAI. I'll get them to help you.

*He goes to open the door and stands waiting. She leaves the
box on the bed and goes out with him.*

26. Interior. Country house. Ballroom. Morning. SIMON,
MILENA *and* BRODOVICH *stand looking out over the grounds
in front of the ballroom windows. They are surrounded by
buckets, and brushes, and two high step-ladders.*

From their point of view:

27. Exterior. Country house. Grounds. NIKOLAI *and* BLANKA, *walking.* BLANKA *has one of* NIKOLAI's *uniform jackets slung over her shoulders.*

28. Interior. Country house. Ballroom. Morning. BRODOVICH *takes one of the ladders and plants it under the great crystal chandelier. Then he gets the other ladder and prepares to clean the windows.* MILENA *starts swabbing the floor.* SIMON *goes to the ladder under the chandelier and drums his fingers on one of the steps.*

SIMON. I see. (*Pause.*) I get the chandelier.

BRODOVICH. You can have the windows if you like. It's a damn sight more work.

SIMON. But less vertiginous.

BRODOVICH. What? At the top?

SIMON. That girl could be my daughter.

BRODOVICH. And the Colonel could be my priest!

SIMON *crosses to* MILENA *and watches her working.*

SIMON. Does one *wash* ballroom floors?

MILENA. Do you expect me to polish it?

BRODOVICH. A nice bit of parquet.

SIMON *crosses to* BRODOVICH, *now on his ladder with a damp cloth.*

SIMON. You can *lean* your ladder. It has *support,* d'you see?

BRODOVICH. Yours has got those cords.

SIMON *goes to his ladder. He looks up at the chandelier, then at the two cords connecting the sides of the ladder. He jabs down the side of his hand on one of them: it breaks. He does the same to the other: it holds.*

SIMON. No good.

BRODOVICH *has been watching him, grinning.*

BRODOVICH. I don't think you've got any choice, Comrade. You raise the Colonel's blood pressure just by existing!

SIMON *rests one elbow on the ladder and ponders.*

SIMON. From the top — I still couldn't reach that chandelier. Don't want to damage it, do we? Looks to me like an irreplaceable piece. Genuine crystal. (*Pause.*) And we don't want to damage Rusakov either.

BRODOVICH *comes down, rinses his cloth, and nimbly climbs the ladder under the chandelier. Half way up:*

SIMON. Bravo!

BRODOVICH. You can get on with the windows.

SIMON. I'll hold this ladder steady for you.

BRODOVICH. I'll break your bloody neck for you!

SIMON *shrugs. He gets a cloth, mounts* BRODOVICH's *ladder. The chandelier tinkles as* BRODOVICH *gingerly works on the crystal pendants. They are dusty, and he sneezes. The whole chandelier is set in motion, tinkling. The ladder sways.* BRODOVICH *can cope — he is one of those people.* SIMON *is perfunctorily mopping at the window.*

SIMON (*somewhat aghast*). Toil! Honest, genuine toil!

BRODOVICH. I bet you can't remember the last time.

SIMON. I understand the nobility of labour. You and I have heard a lot about it, haven't we, Brodovich? Who else but the Communist Party would glorify the most notoriously hated activity in human experience? (*He peers down at* MILENA.) But don't misunderstand me, Miss Milena. Salvation through suffering is a Russian obsession. As in everything else which bears on the suppression of joy, the Bolsheviks are not original. Thousands of cockeyed Russian holy men have been peddling the idea for centuries. (*Pause.*) *True joy,* if you understand me, is supposed to be achieved through humility and service to one's fellows. That's where the spiritual catch comes in. Before you know where you are, humility is humiliation and service is servitude. I wrote to Stalin along those lines once, when tight as a tick. But had the presence of mind to burn the letter.

BRODOVICH. Are you saying the Party's no better than the Tsars? And the Orthodox Church?

SIMON. I can see you have more than mincemeat between your ears, Brodovich. You divine my message. I'm crazy. I'm one of those that mentally speaking got away. I don't want to go into the politics in general. It's my own case that fascinates me. I'm an egoist, thank God. Look at that crystal! How it shines! (*Pause.*) I look on that girl as if she were my very own daughter. If Beneš doesn't lose all his marbles in Kosice, she has a wonderful life in front of her.

MILENA *has been working hard, occasionally paying attention. Now she throws down her mop.*

MILENA. She has, has she?

SIMON. I'm not insensitive to her . . . to her *condition.*

MILENA. Well then?

SIMON. Forgive me. Do you know what *some* people have experienced these last five years?

MILENA. It's Blanka we're talking about.

SIMON. I will say. I hope she doesn't have the added misfortune of falling in love with Shchetkin. I'd get irrational. I'd have to do something. The man's a criminal. Even Brodovich's line is at least straightforward rape. No attempt to dress things up. (*Pause.*) To dissemble tender feelings. (*Pause.*) And anyway he's under Shchetkin's thumb. (*Pause.*) But the Colonel can be a charmer. I know. He used to charm me, when he was a student. When he wasn't insulting me.

MILENA. She should go to America. Her uncle has a factory. Now *he* got out when those pigs marched into the Sudetanland. She should go to America and take me with her.

SIMON. Ah, America —

MILENA. And what do you know about it?

SIMON. One dreams, Madam. One dreams.

MILENA. I can't see you making your way there. Not by any means I can't.

SIMON. Some small mid-Western college, you know? Gracious buildings. A quiet campus. The odd bell tolling somewhere, as one bends over one's books of an evening. (*Pause.*) Baseball.

MILENA. I'd look after her.

SIMON. Phi Beta Kapa. Drum majorettes. Hollywood. Martinis. (*Pause.*) Er — pastrami. Bagels. Slinky women. (*Pause.*) Er —

MILENA. She'll need someone to look after her.

SIMON. Ice-cold martinis at faculty parties. Deferential students. (*Pause.*) Professor Rusakov, whose course on the decline of Soviet literature and the myth of social realism is a savage indictment of the fate of the arts in that country —

He stops. BRODOVICH is staring at him pityingly from his ladder. SIMON scuttles down his own ladder. Goes to BRODOVICH's and kicks it. It sways perilously, BRODOVICH loses his balance and falls off.

SIMON. Hit me then. Go on. Go on. Hit me.

BRODOVICH comes towards him with fist raised. SIMON sinks into a squatting position and starts crying.

SIMON. Dear old Brodovich. Comrade. I didn't mean to bring you down. It was your expression. The look in your eyes. It was all of miserable, misguided, wretched Russia staring out at me. The envy. The malice. The contempt. The violence. The cruelty. The —

He yelps as BRODOVICH kicks him hard in the backside and goes back to his ladder. SIMON drags himself to his feet, affecting wounded dignity. BRODOVICH wags a finger at him as he climbs up once more.

BRODOVICH. It'll be the firing squad for you. (*He spits.*) Education! (BRODOVICH *goes on working at the chandelier.*) Look at him! A mousefart with a diploma —

SIMON (*shouting*). Toe-rag!

BRODOVICH. D'you want my boot up your arse, again, Comrade?

SIMON (*shouting*). Of course I do! Come on. Come on down and kick me again —

He bends down with his backside pointing in BRODOVICH's direction. BRODOVICH is grinning. SIMON jabs at his backside with his thumb.

SIMON. I dare you. I invite you.

He turns towards BRODOVICH and sinks to his knees with his hands pressed together.

SIMON. I *beg* you —

BRODOVICH shakes his head wonderingly, and goes on

cleaning the chandelier. MILENA *goes and stands over the
supplicant* RUSAKOV.

MILENA. Aren't you ashamed of yourself?

SIMON (*rising, dusting his knees*). The free spirit, in its travail . . .
dear lady . . . craves humiliation as the baby puckers its
tiny lips round the nipple. You think Blanka is a trifle
cuckoo? Let me tell you she is a novice. An unformed
beginner. Rusakov has been slowly pickling in insanity since
nineteen-nineteen. Things have been building up, I assure
you. A rare old head of steam! It's a wonder it hasn't blown
my ears off before now. It's true that history is a mighty
antagonist, but most people do not exactly have a historical
view of themselves. No. The still, small flame of the individual
soul, Madam — is trying to illuminate its own humble patch.
There were plenty of so-called divine fools in the time of the
Tsars. But your Rusakovs, I must insist on explaining, they
rejoice in an even higher form of idiocy. They aspire to
sainthood in the absence of a religion. Their little stub of a
candle burns even in windbags like me. We have to be crass,
and abject, and unselfseeking. We have to inflate ourselves
and strut and posture. Because we have so much to hide
that we can only take refuge in the grotesque. I *want*
Brodovich's boot. I *love* Brodovich's boot. It inspires me.
If I were musical I'd sing songs to it. If surrealism were
permitted in our country I'd exhibit Brodovich's boot in
a pisspot. (*Pause.*) Watch —

Again he kneels down with his backside pointing towards
BRODOVICH — *whose rage has been mounting throughout*
SIMON's *peroration. He comes down from the ladder and
kicks the proffered behind.*
    SIMON *shuffles towards the door on hands and knees,
squeaking and suffering himself to be kicked all the way.*
    MILENA, *quite overawed, watches the spectacle in silence.*
    BRODOVICH *returns looking pleased with himself.*

BRODOVICH. Don't look so shocked. It's the only way to
treat them.

MILENA. 'Them'?

BRODOVICH. You find them all over the place.

MILENA. In Russia?

BRODOVICH. In the Soviet Union.

MILENA. Poor man!

BRODOVICH. They spend their lives crawling through the loopholes.

MILENA. *What* loopholes?

BRODOVICH. In the system.

MILENA. But how can you treat him like that?

BRODOVICH. Didn't he ask me? Didn't he provoke me?

MILENA. I suppose so. But after all. He's not all there. Is he?

BRODOVICH. Oh, he's all there all right!

MILENA. Well he has a funny way of *being* all there.

BRODOVICH. It's just the dregs of the *old* system, d'you see?

MILENA. No.

BRODOVICH. And he's relying on Colonel Shchetkin to get him out of it.

MILENA. Out of what?

BRODOVICH. He's not just an old wandering drunk you know. He's a deserter.

MILENA. A deserting cook?

BRODOVICH. Cooks are notoriously gun-shy.

MILENA. Isn't everybody?

BRODOVICH. Well cooks are.

> *Pause.*

MILENA. And what's to become of Blanka and me?

29. Exterior. Country house grounds. Morning. *On a hill overlooking a dusty road,* BLANKA *and* NIKOLAI.
> *From their point of view:*

30. Exterior. Country road. Morning. *The* DRUNKEN SOLDIER *with the bicycle is hanging precariously on the cross arm of a telegraph pole, holding on by clutching the insulators. His bike is propped at the foot of the pole.*

31. Exterior. Country house grounds. Morning. NIKOLAI *stands shading his eyes and squinting at the scene below. He turns to* BLANKA.

NIKOLAI. You see that Red Army soldier down there?

BLANKA. He looks as if he's going to drop off.

    NIKOLAI *pulls binoculars from a case and trains them on the* SOLDIER.

NIKOLAI. It's one of my men.

    BLANKA *starts giggling.*

NIKOLAI. He's supposed to be what we call 'restoring communications'.

    The SOLDIER *falls off the telegraph pole and lies inert in the grass.*

BLANKA. Shouldn't we go down?

NIKOLAI. I don't think so.

BLANKA. What if he's hurt?

NIKOLAI. It's unlikely.

BLANKA. But you don't know —

NIKOLAI. I doubt it.

    Pause.

BLANKA. Where are the others?

NIKOLAI. He's drunk. Look at him. He's got a bottle now.

    He hands her the binoculars, which she trains on the SOLDIER.

BLANKA. Where are the others?

NIKOLAI. What others?

BLANKA. Soldiers.

NIKOLAI. There won't be any. (*Pause.*) Yet.

BLANKA. It's not possible.

NIKOLAI. The whole district is in a kind of — quarantine. I don't know how else to describe it.

    Pause.

BLANKA. I don't understand.

NIKOLAI. Nothing mysterious.

BLANKA. I didn't think the end of the war would be like this.

NIKOLAI. It isn't the end of the war.

He walks on, and after hesitating a moment she follows.

32. Exterior. Country house grounds. Lake. Morning. *We open on a high view of the lake, encircled by trees. A small boat in the centre of the lake, not moving. In it:* NIKOLAI *and* BLANKA.

33. Exterior. Lake. Boat. Morning. NIKOLAI *and* BLANKA *sit opposite each other, hugging their knees.*

NIKOLAI. Well it's too cold to swim today.

BLANKA. Even in the winter, I used to.

NIKOLAI. You should see Leningrad when the Neva is frozen. The sun sparkles on the snow and ice. On the spires and domes —

Pause.

BLANKA. I'm frightened.

Pause.

NIKOLAI. That's what Rusakov said to me yesterday. When I found him in his ditch. (*He laughs.*) He expected to be arrested. (*Pause.*) Then he saw it was his old friend Nikolai. And started calculating.

BLANKA. I *am* frightened.

NIKOLAI. But not like Simon. Not of me.

BLANKA. It wasn't like this when the Germans came.

NIKOLAI. It isn't typical of us, either.

BLANKA. I have that feeling you get in the summer when you're waiting for a thunderstorm. When everything gets glassy, and heavy.

NIKOLAI. Fanciful!

Pause.

BLANKA. I'm cold now.

NIKOLAI. I'll row us back soon.

BLANKA. Why did we come out on the lake?

NIKOLAI. Didn't you suggest it?

BLANKA. You did.

NIKOLAI. There's a special intensity about moments of peace in wartime.

Pause.

BLANKA. You want to question me, don't you?

NIKOLAI. Do I?

BLANKA. You want to make love to me.

NIKOLAI. Do I?

BLANKA. You don't know whether I know anything.

NIKOLAI. That's true.

BLANKA. Whether you'd be taking advantage of me.

NIKOLAI. I wouldn't wish to do that.

BLANKA. Those religious peasants I told you about. It didn't stop them rutting.

NIKOLAI. You could hardly be ignorant about sex, after all.

BLANKA. My mother saw to it I was told. (*Pause.*) And then there is one's body.

She smiles bleakly.

BLANKA. Milena says the Red Army is raping and looting everywhere. That your soldiers are barbaric.

NIKOLAI. I suppose neither better nor worse than any other conquering army. The Germans devastated Russia. The troops are bitter and angry. Their privations, their sufferings have been beyond endurance.

BLANKA. But we are not the enemy.

NIKOLAI (*drily*). We are still a very backward country.

BLANKA. A wild, stinking horde of dangerous animals — Milena said. (*Pause.*) The Americans wouldn't be like that, she said.

NIKOLAI. Oh, the Americans won't rape. They'll buy. Our Tartars and Mongols violate. The Americans negotiate. No wonder their best-known cigarettes are called Lucky Strike!

BLANKA. So you defend your men!

NIKOLAI. I think the cultural and moral condition of our
soldiers is — disgusting. (*He grins.*) Give us another fifty
years! We shall try to improve.

Pause.

BLANKA. I am a little in love with you, Nikolai.

Pause.

NIKOLAI. And I with you.

They lean towards each other and kiss, very gently. And as
BLANKA *moves back:*

BLANKA. But it isn't sex.

NIKOLAI. It has to be that too.

Pause.

BLANKA. I shall kill myself if the Nazis take you away.

Pause.

NIKOLAI. The — Nazis?

He is jolted, staring at her now expressionless face.

BLANKA. What did I say?

Pause.

NIKOLAI. Nothing.

BLANKA *is suddenly laughing and clapping her hands*
together.

BLANKA. We will have a dinner party tonight? Won't we?

NIKOLAI. I promise.

BLANKA. And funny Simon Rusakov too?

NIKOLAI. Him too.

She leans back holding the side of the boat, holding her face
to the sky and laughing. NIKOLAI *begins to row towards the*
shore.

34. Interior. Country house. Ballroom. Evening. *A long highly-*
polished table set with fine glass and china, silver cutlery, a large
bowl of flowers. The elaborateness of the setting contrasts with

*the remains of what has been a sparse meal. Most of the glasses
and cutlery is unused. Candles burn in branched candelabra.
Above the table, the chandelier gives a dim soft glow, shot with
reflections from the myriad pendants of crystal. Three places
at the table have been set and used.*

*RUSAKOV sits at one of the long sides, slumped forward, his
head on his arms. There is a cluster of empty bottles in front of
him.*

*NIKOLAI and BLANKA are dancing to the gramophone —
another thirties' waltz. BLANKA is in a lovely chiffon dress of
the pre-war period. The record stops. BLANKA and NIKOLAI
go on dancing. SIMON stirs. He rests his elbows on the table
and cups his chin in his hands, watching. Suddenly he pipes
up in a clear tenor voice:*

SIMON (*singing*).
  Meshugge Mama,
  Meshugge Papa,
  Meshugge die ganz Familie — (*He fills his wine glass and
  raises it to them.*) Gesundheit!

  *BLANKA crosses to him, snatches the glass and throws it on
  the floor where it smashes.*

BLANKA. Not in German!

  *Nodding, RUSAKOV fills another glass and sits brooding over
  it. BLANKA and NIKOLAI sit opposite each other facing
  down the length of the table. SIMON wags his finger at
  NIKOLAI.*

SIMON. As long as I was sober Nikolai, I didn't want to spoil
  your fun. (*Pause.*) Have I said a word this evening? Have I
  said one single word?

NIKOLAI. It's made a very agreeable change.

SIMON. Shall I spoil your fun? Old aparatchik?

NIKOLAI. You can always try.

SIMON. Shall I spoil his fun, Blanka? (*She stares back at him
  in stony silence.*) Brodovich is drunk, you know. Back there
  in the kitchen. Brodovich too.

NIKOLAI. Oh yes?

SIMON. I let him humiliate me this afternoon. (*Pause.*) This
  morning.

NIKOLAI. We all know you're irresistible.

SIMON. Oh, he's been cockahoop ever since.

NIKOLAI. It's a tendency he has whenever the opposition is puny. I'm ashamed of you, Simon. Picking on a bully like that!

Pause. SIMON *picks up his glass and begins to pace up and down along the table, glancing from one to the other.*

SIMON. The thing is, Blanka. You see, according to Brodovich this house is going to be an interrogation centre. (*Pause.*) Well that's a relatively polite name for it. (*Pause.*) I should think 'execution centre' might be a more appropriate term. *That's* what my gifted ex-pupil is here to set up.

Pause.

BLANKA (*to* NIKOLAI). To interrogate whom?

NIKOLAI. Brodovich is lying.

SIMON. Boasting.

NIKOLAI. Pure fantasy.

SIMON. He sweats with excitement when he talks about it.

BLANKA (*loudly, almost hysterical*). To interrogate whom?

SIMON. Who else but the enemies of the Soviet Union? The Communist Party. The State. The inviolate wisdom of Comrade Stalin. Oh, there's an endless list of things one can turn out to be an enemy of, in our country. (*Pause.*) And having discovered revolutionary justice, you can be sure we shall export it to Poland and Czechoslovakia. Hungary and Roumania. And so on and so on. But that's all by the way. (*He refills his glass.*) I mean. I've sat here all evening and watched you two dancing. Gazing into each other's eyes. (*He pulls out his revolver and shoots one of the crystal pendants in the chandelier.*) She loves him. (*He shoots another.*) She loves him not.

The shots echo loudly. The chandelier is tinkling. Smiling amiably, SIMON *sits down with his revolver in front of him and drinks.*

NIKOLAI. Put that damned gun away! (*Pause: shouting.*) Brodovich —

SIMON. Brodovich has gone. He's gone looking for a woman.

I'm sure you understand, don't you, Nikolai?

NIKOLAI. Give me that gun —

SIMON (*picking up the gun*). There now. That's what we call an impasse.

He drains his glass and refills it. BLANKA *suddenly stands up screaming.*

BLANKA. *Stop it!*

SIMON *looks up at the chandelier and smiles at* NIKOLAI.

SIMON. You used to be a bit of a gambler, Nikolai. What about: the one who gets the last crystal pendant gets the girl?

Pause.

NIKOLAI. He's mad.

SIMON. Come come. You don't want *her*. You *want* her.

NIKOLAI *raises his gun slowly and shoots a pendant.*

NIKOLAI. What about: the last one to shoot the last pendant — gets the next shot?

NIKOLAI *is drinking too, now.* BLANKA *looks from one to the other in disbelief.*

BLANKA. Nikolai!

NIKOLAI. Sit down or get out.

His tone freezes her. She sits — stiff-backed, trembling.

BLANKA. Is it true? What he said about this house? (*Pause.*) And *you?*

Pause.

NIKOLAI. Your Dr Beneš will compromise with us. He has little choice. (*Pause.*) But there are always misguided individuals who will try to resist. (*Pause.*) We have our policy.

Pause.

BLANKA. So did the Nazis.

SIMON. Oh dear me. You mustn't say things like that. It's most undialectical. Tell her, Nikolai. Tell her the difference between Nazi atrocities and Communist atrocities. Tell her the difference between Communist freedom and bourgeois freedom. Tell her how the meaning of words is miraculously transformed according to your point of view. (*He smiles benignly at* BLANKA.) He was always something of an ideological wizard.

NIKOLAI. Blanka —

SIMON *shoots the chandelier again.*

SIMON. But we shouldn't delude ourselves that he believes in anything. (*Pause.*) So how can he be as he is? (*Pause.*) I doubt if he's cruel by nature. He isn't one of those sadists who are ready to serve any régime that can feed him victims. He's not some mediocrity trying to compensate with power for his lack of gifts. One can't point a finger at the Shchetkins and say: he's been conditioned, he's been mystified, he's a kind of political psychopath. The Shchetkins are by no means either fooled by the system or slaves to it. (*He smiles.*) It's true that mediocrity rises to the surface in Russia, like scum in a cesspool. But Nikolai is brilliant. And not insensitive. (*To* BLANKA.) I do believe he is in love as well!

SIMON *dispenses with his glass and drinks from the bottle.* NIKOLAI *is flushed with anger, drinking rapidly. He pulls open the collar of his tunic.* BLANKA *sits with her head lowered, picking at her dress.*

NIKOLAI (*very quietly*). Is the professor in love too? (*Pause.*) What a drunken, sweaty, pathetic creature you are, Simon! (*Pause.*) Clinging to survival. And flaunting it. And dressing up self-loathing as self-mockery. And sidestepping any kind of responsibility for anything. (*Pause.*) You won't be a survivor of this war. At best you'll be a sordid remnant. A moral scarecrow. (*He raises his gun to the chandelier with both hands, squinting along the barrel: fires.*) A gibbering eunuch. (*Fires again.*) A squeaking bag of sexual envy, not least of all!

The two men are staring at each other, fascinated by each other. This kind of hatred is a form of exhilaration. BLANKA *lifts her face to* NIKOLAI *slowly:*

BLANKA. And you propose . . . to do your obscene work . . . in this house! (*She beats the table violently with clenched fists.*) He *kissed* me! (*She scrubs at her lips with the back of her hand.*) He's shit! He shit on my *mouth!* I swallowed him. He's inside me!

There is a long silence broken only by her sobbing.

NIKOLAI. Oh, what have you done — Rusakov!

Pause.

SIMON. She has to know.

Pause.

NIKOLAI. What?

SIMON. The truth.

NIKOLAI. Ah! You have the truth?

SIMON. The facts.

NIKOLAI. But you dream of having her yourself.

SIMON. No.

NIKOLAI. Liar.

Pause.

SIMON. I've always wanted to ask one of you people —

NIKOLAI. Yes?

SIMON. How you can torment and degrade others.

NIKOLAI. Perhaps we're insane.

SIMON. Soviet reality!

Pause.

NIKOLAI. I rather enjoy your hatred, you know.

SIMON. Because you're handsome and powerful and self-confident? Because you are secure and privileged? (*Pause.*) Or because you're devoid of feeling.

NIKOLAI. You surely don't think these things matter in relation to the prisoners, do you?

SIMON. You enjoy my hatred because as soon as I show it, I'm guilty. (*Pause.*) And my hatred of you is really my own shame burning itself out. (*Pause.*) What I feel for you is the accumulation of everything I've seen and heard, every rumour, every whisper . . . each missing colleague, friend, relative . . . and the thousands of anonymous ghosts haunting Russia. (*He stumbles and leans over* NIKOLAI.) And I dare not even kill you!

SIMON *whirls round and empties his gun at the chandelier. As the noise echoes and dies away, he stands leaning with both hands on the table looking at* BLANKA.

SIMON (*quietly*). For more than fifteen years.

*Pause. BLANKA takes a fork. Slowly and methodically she
makes tears in her dress. The two men watch her shredding
the rich material as if engaged in some ancient ritual of grief.*

NIKOLAI. Semyon Vasilievich — (SIMON *turns slowly and
looks at him.*) There is no secret.

SIMON. If I were your prisoner —

NIKOLAI But you *are* my prisoner!

Pause.

SIMON. And she?

NIKOLAI. Now I'm afraid she *is* insane. Don't you think?
(BLANKA *runs out of the room.*) I can't tell you how I've
achieved my extraordinary detachment. I haven't the faintest
idea. (*Pause.*) I agree with just about everything you say.
(*Pause.*) Did I even turn my head when she ran out? (*Pause.*)
You all *collaborate* so! It isn't only because you are helpless.

*He looks up at the chandelier now reduced to a near-skeleton
of what it was. He changes the magazine in his gun.*

NIKOLAI. Shall we finish that absurd thing *off*? (*He shoots at
the chandelier rapidly, smiling.*) A sweet child. Another
casualty.

Pause.

SIMON. When do your people move in?

NIKOLAI (*grinning*). When the telephone rings. (*Pause.*) You
wouldn't know — I suppose — that General Patton's forces
are in Western Bohemia? (*Pause.*) Does that stir your
imagination?

SIMON *drops wearily into* BLANKA's *chair. The two face
each other across the table, across the debris of the
chandelier. Each has a bottle in one hand and a gun in the
other.*

SIMON. You win.

Pause.

NIKOLAI. Do I? Win what? And why?

Pause.

SIMON. I suppose the old woman is looking after the girl —

NIKOLAI. I suppose so. (*Pause.*) How do I win, Simon?

> BLANKA *enters, clutching her cardboard box.* MILENA *follows apprehensively.* BLANKA *turns a chair away from the table and sits rocking and crooning over the box. Occasionally she looks back over her shoulder at* SIMON *or* NIKOLAI. *Her eyes are quite blank.*
> SIMON *goes and kneels in front of her.*

SIMON. What's in your box, Blanka?

MILENA. *No!*

> BLANKA *is giggling.*

SIMON. What's in there?

> *She suddenly upends the box, pulling off the lid. A stream of fine grey ash pours to the floor.* BLANKA *looks at* SIMON, *giggling.*

BLANKA. My father. (*With an insanely confiding leer.*) It's . . . my . . . father.

> *She drops to her knees, taking a handful of ash. She lets it trickle through her fingers.*
> SIMON *turns away, goes back to the table.* NIKOLAI *is squinting along the barrel of his gun — at nothing.*

NIKOLAI (*softly*). Your brain is addled, Rusakov. (*Pause.*) Your impressive moral outrage is acutely embarrassing. (*Pause.*) You aren't even a woolly idealist. Nothing so disarming. Everything about you is ambiguous. (*Pause.*) Just now for example. You knew what was in the box. Do you *know* what kind of point you were trying to make? (*Pause.*) Look at her. (BLANKA *is crooning over the ashes.*) Listen to her. What on *earth* kind of confusion are you *in?* You disappoint me, you really do. We are not antagonists. We are complementary. You might try asking yourself where we'd be without each other. It didn't all simply begin with Stalin. Or Lenin. It's been there all the time. We have the most intimate relationship imaginable, you and I. (*Pause.*) Could we *exist* without each other? (*Pause.*) I often look into the eyes of men like you during the long nights we share in prison, and think: the fellow knows that by any decent standards he is a morally superior being. (*Pause.*) But how would he know that if I were not here? (*Pause.*) I don't have a *meaning* in the scheme of things. I have a modest *function* — d'you see? Is that plain? Isn't that honest? The amazing thing is not that we are so depraved — but that you are. Every single one of the thousands of Rusakovs. (*He smiles condescendingly.*) Don't look so anguished! The next generation of Rusakovs will speak for you. You'll all be canonised in the West one way or another. And those who get out will thunder from their lofty moral pulpits. *Your* predicament is just that you haven't the courage to raise your voice. You'll never be heard. (*Pause.*) And you can't forgive yourself. (*Pause.*) Your ego needs it.

> *There is a long silence.* RUSAKOV *is as if blinded for a moment* NIKOLAI *puts a cigarette between his lips and lights it.* BLANKA *croons on and on.* MILENA *has her arms round her.*
> SIMON *shoots* NIKOLAI *between the eyes. He stands and bows to* MILENA, *with a crazy look.*

SIMON. Semyon Vasilievich Rusakov. (*Pause.*) At your service.

> MILENA *has* BLANKA *by the shoulders and is backing her away towards the door.*

MILENA. Lieutenant — (*Pause.*) Lieutenant? (*Pause.*) I didn't see anything. I promise you.

> *Pause.*

SIMON. Oh but I did. (*Pause.*) I saw that I really have always envied him.

> *He sits down, still holding his gun.* MILENA *gets* BLANKA *out of the room.* SIMON *changes the magazine in his gun and sits idly shooting what remains of the chandelier.*

Fade out.